STRATEGIES for Writers

Level C

Authors

Leslie W. Crawford, Ed.D.
Georgia College & State University

Rebecca Bowers Sipe, Ed.D.
Eastern Michigan University

ZB
Zaner-Bloser

Educational Consultants

Barbara Marinak
Reading Supervisor
Mechanicsburg, PA

Catherine C. Thome, Ed.D.
English/Language Arts and Assessment Coordinator
Educational Services Division
Lake County Regional Office of Education
Grayslake, IL

Science Content Reviewer

Michael Grote, Ed.D.
Math and Science Education
Columbus Public Schools
Columbus, OH

Teacher Reviewers

Janice Andrus, Chanhassen, MN
Shannon Basner, Hollis, NY
Teressa D. Bell, Nashville, TN
Victoria B. Casady, Ferguson, MO
Kristin Cashman, Mechanicsburg, PA
Jeanie Denaro, Brooklyn, NY
Susan H. Friedman, Ph.D., Sharon, PA
Katherine Harrington, Mechanicsburg, PA
Dianna L. Hinderer, Ypsilanti, MI

Eleanor Kane, Stow, OH
Jean Kochevar, Minneapolis, MN
Diane L. Nicholson, Pittsburgh, PA
Susan Peery, San Antonio, TX
David Philpot, San Francisco, CA
Jodi Ramos, San Antonio, TX
Jacqueline Sullivan, Sunnyvale, CA
Rita Warden-Short, Brentwood, TN
Roberta M. Wykoff, Stow, OH

Page Design Concepts and Cover Design

Tommaso Design Group

Photo Credits

Models: George C. Anderson Photography

p11, Joe McDonald, CORBIS; p17, Michele Westmorland, Getty Images; p21, George C. Anderson; p35, Steve Dunwell Photography, Getty Images; pp49, 65, 157, 222, Getty Images, PhotoDisc; p55, Annie Griffith Belt, CORBIS; p73, PhotoDisc; p93, Andy Caufield, Getty Images; p111, John Kelly, Getty Images; p121, Philip Habib, Getty Images; p131, Dennis Degnan, CORBIS; pp175, 181, CORBIS; p201, R. Derek Smith, Getty Images; p221, Stephen Webster, Worldwide Hideout, Inc.

Art Credits

p21, George C. Anderson; pp58, 96, Linda Bittner; p80, CD Hullinger; pp137, 138, 145, 146, 147, Heidi Chang; pp149, 150, 151, Anthony Davila; p162, Karen Stormer-Brooks. HB5, HB9, HB10, HB11, HB13, HB18, HB20, HB21, HB26, HB27, HB34, Marilyn Rodgers Bahney Paselsky; HB14, HB19, Brooke Albrecht.

Production, Photo Research, and Art Buying by Inkwell Publishing Solutions, Inc.

ISBN 0-7367-1233-X

Zaner-Bloser, Inc., P.O. Box 16764, Columbus, Ohio 43216-6764 (1-800-421-3018)

Printed in the United States of America   06   104   9 8 7 6

NARRATIVE

writing

DESCRIPTIVE
writing

EXPOSITORY

writing

NARRATIVE

writing

PERSUASIVE

writing

writing

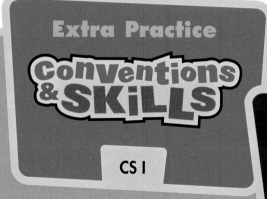

Extra Practice

Conventions & SKiLLS

CS 1

Writer's HandBook

HB 1

NARRATIVE

writing

narrates something to the reader.

1

Personal Narrative

2

Friendly Letter

NARRATIVE writing

Personal Narrative

In this chapter, you will work with one kind of narrative writing: a **personal narrative**.

A **personal narrative** is a true story about something that the writer saw or did. It describes a real experience that the author had.

Read the questions below. Then read the personal narrative paragraph on the next page. Keep the questions in mind as you read.

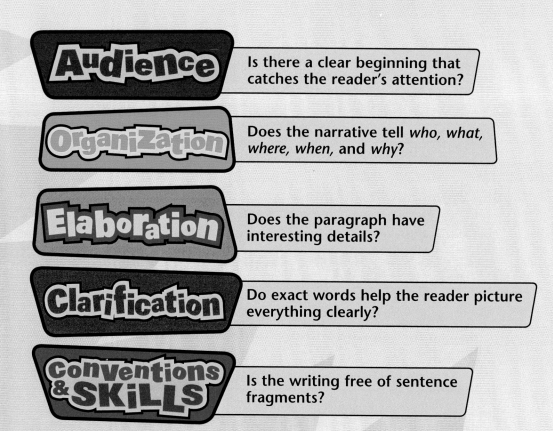

Audience — Is there a clear beginning that catches the reader's attention?

Organization — Does the narrative tell *who, what, where, when,* and *why?*

Elaboration — Does the paragraph have interesting details?

Clarification — Do exact words help the reader picture everything clearly?

Conventions & Skills — Is the writing free of sentence fragments?

A WHOLE BAT-TALION

by Luis Delgado

Did you know that bats have lived in Carlsbad Caverns for more than 5,000 years? That is what the park ranger told us as I sat in the outdoor theater with my brother Mario. Our parents had just driven us across the desert to see an amazing event. Now, as we waited, we listened to the ranger at Carlsbad Caverns National Park. She explained that more than 300,000 Mexican free-tailed bats live in the cave. "During the day, the bats sleep," she said, "but they get hungry, and at night they come out to eat. Every night they eat tons of insects!" The sun went down as the ranger finished talking, and then it happened. First, it looked like a puff of smoke coming from the cave. Then it seemed more like a spinning black tornado. Waves of bats poured out of the cave. As the bats flew in circles, darting and looping higher and higher, we heard a soft clicking sound. I never knew there were so many bats living so close to my home. I'm glad they are all eating harmful insects while we sleep!

Using a Rubric

A rubric is a tool that helps you assess a piece of writing. It can also help you figure out if your own writing still needs more work.

How do you use a rubric? You assign 1, 2, 3, or 4 points to tell how well you or another writer did certain things.

Remember the questions you read on page 10? Those questions were used to make this rubric.

> Hi! My name is Isabel. I'm learning how to write a personal narrative, too. What did you think of the personal narrative paragraph you just read? Look at this rubric. First, read each question. Next, read the information for each question. Then we'll use the rubric to assess the personal narrative.

Audience

Is there a clear beginning that catches the reader's attention?

Organization

Does the narrative tell *who, what, where, when,* and *why?*

Elaboration

Does the paragraph have interesting details?

Clarification

Do exact words help the reader picture everything clearly?

Conventions & Skills

Is the writing free of sentence fragments?

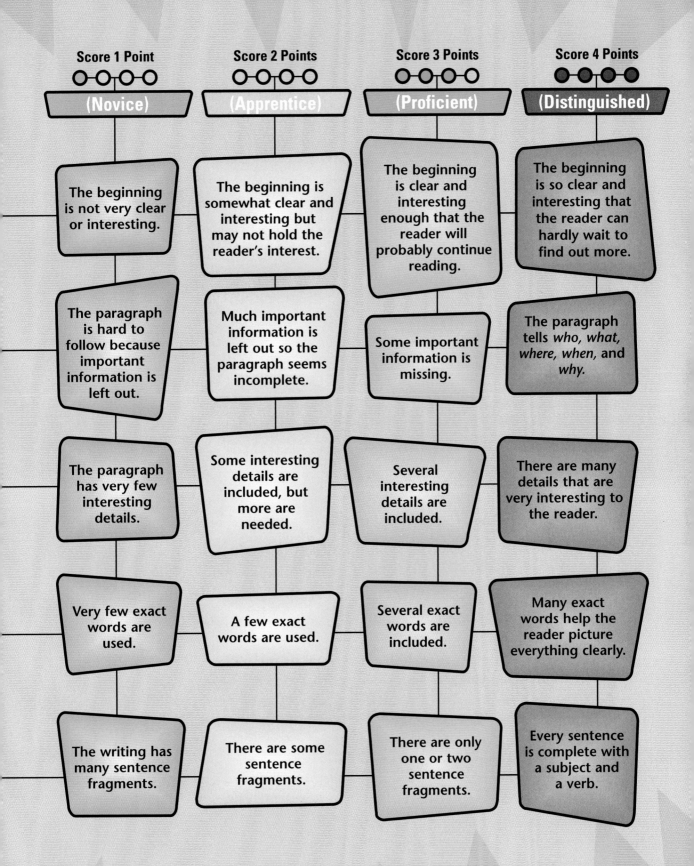

Score 1 Point (Novice)	Score 2 Points (Apprentice)	Score 3 Points (Proficient)	Score 4 Points (Distinguished)
The beginning is not very clear or interesting.	The beginning is somewhat clear and interesting but may not hold the reader's interest.	The beginning is clear and interesting enough that the reader will probably continue reading.	The beginning is so clear and interesting that the reader can hardly wait to find out more.
The paragraph is hard to follow because important information is left out.	Much important information is left out so the paragraph seems incomplete.	Some important information is missing.	The paragraph tells *who*, *what*, *where*, *when*, and *why*.
The paragraph has very few interesting details.	Some interesting details are included, but more are needed.	Several interesting details are included.	There are many details that are very interesting to the reader.
Very few exact words are used.	A few exact words are used.	Several exact words are included.	Many exact words help the reader picture everything clearly.
The writing has many sentence fragments.	There are some sentence fragments.	There are only one or two sentence fragments.	Every sentence is complete with a subject and a verb.

Using a Rubric
to Study the Model

Discuss each question in the rubric with your classmates. Find words and sentences in the personal narrative paragraph that help you answer each one. Use the rubric to give Luis Delgado's personal narrative a score for each question.

Is there a clear beginning that catches the reader's attention?

"I know from the first sentence that I will be reading about bats that live in a cave. This sentence makes the topic of the paragraph clear. The writer catches my attention right away by starting with a question that has a surprising fact in it. It makes me want to keep reading to find out more about the bats."

Did you know that bats have lived in Carlsbad Caverns for more than 5,000 years?

Does the narrative tell *who, what, where, when,* **and** *why?*

" Yes, the writer includes details that answer each of those questions. I read through the paper again and found all of these details. These details give me a full understanding of the story. "

Who **was there?**	the author and his brother
What **happened?**	Thousands of bats left a cave.
When **did it happen?**	at sunset
Where **did it happen?**	at Carlsbad Caverns National Park
Why **did it happen?**	The bats wanted insects to eat.

Does the paragraph have interesting details?

" Yes, the paragraph has many interesting details. These details really help me see the bats! Here are two that I really like. "

First, it looked like a puff of smoke coming from the cave. Then it seemed more like a spinning black tornado.

Do exact words help the reader picture everything clearly?

" The author uses many exact words to help me see clear pictures. For example, he uses the word **poured** instead of a less exact word like **came**. The word **looping** is a better choice than the word **going**. "

Waves of bats poured out of the cave. As the bats flew in circles, darting and looping higher and higher, we heard a soft clicking sound.

 Conventions & SKiLLS

Is the writing free of sentence fragments?

Every sentence has a subject and a verb, which means that there are no sentence fragments. Here is an example of a complete sentence.

"Every night they eat tons of insects!"

Now it's my turn to write!

I'm going to write my own personal narrative paragraph. Follow along to see how I use the model and the rubric to practice good writing strategies.

Isabel

Writer of a Personal Narrative Paragraph

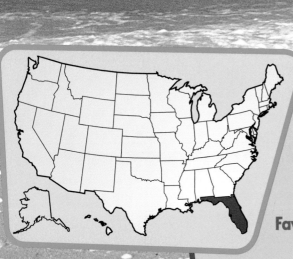

Name: Isabel

Home: Florida

Hobbies: swimming, reading, collecting shells

Favorite Book: *The Magic School Bus on the Ocean Floor* by Joanna Cole

Assignment: personal narrative paragraph

Prewriting

Gather

Think about something that I saw or did. Jot notes about my experience.

> I love to collect shells. Last winter, my aunt took me to Sanibel Island to find some. Sanibel is in Florida on the Gulf of Mexico. It is famous for having beautiful seashells.
>
> "My teacher asked everyone to write a personal narrative paragraph. I tried to think of something I did that I really enjoyed. I decided to write about my trip to collect shells. The trip was so much fun! I thought my friends might enjoy reading about it, too. I'll start by jotting down some notes about what happened that day.

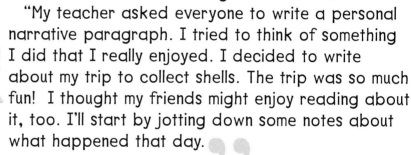

Finding Shells on Sanibel Island

- went with Aunt Angela to Sanibel Island
- big storm washed up lots of shells
- looked on beach for shells for my collection
- found many kinds

Go to page 6 in the **Practice** the Strategy **Notebook!**

Prewriting

Organize
Use my notes to make a 5 W's chart.

> I know from the **Rubric** that my paragraph needs to be organized. It should have details that tell who, what, where, when, and why. The details will help readers understand what happened on my trip to collect shells.
>
> "I can use the notes I just wrote to make a 5 W's Chart. That way I'll be sure I didn't leave out any important information. Then I'll use the chart when I draft my personal narrative paragraph.

5 W's Chart

A **5 W's chart** helps organize information. A writer can use the chart to ask and answer these questions: *Who? What? Where? When? Why?*

My 5 W's Chart

Who was there?	Aunt Angela and I
What happened?	found lots of seashells
Where did it happen?	a beach on Sanibel Island
When did it happen?	after a big storm
Why did it happen?	wanted to find different shells for my collection

Go to page 8 in the **Practice** the Strategy **Notebook!**

Drafting

Write

Draft my personal narrative. Make sure it has a good beginning.

" Now I'm ready to write. I know from the **Rubric** that my paragraph needs a clear beginning that will catch the reader's attention. The beginning is sometimes called a lead. The lead often gives an idea of what the paragraph will be about. I will try writing three different leads and then see which one I like best. "

Lead

The **lead** is the first sentence of a paper. A good lead grabs the reader's attention and makes the reader want to read more. The lead might give a surprising fact, ask a question, or tell what someone said.

Surprise Lead: I found a buttercup and a lion's paw at the beach.

Question Lead: Is it a good idea to go to the beach after a storm?

Quotation Lead: "What a beautiful shell that is!" Aunt Angela said.

" I'll use my 5 W's chart to help me as I write the rest of my draft. I'll do my best with grammar and spelling, but I can check for mistakes later. I'll write to get my ideas down now. "

Going on a Treasure Hunt

Isabel's lead

→ Is it a good idea to go to the beach after a storm?

It is if you want to find seashells! Aunt Angela ~~and me~~ took
me to a beach on Sanibel Island after a big storm. It was
a great time to hunt for nice shells for my collection. The wind
~~made~~ and waves from the storm made the shells on the
ocean floor loose. Then the shells washed up on the beach.
I walked carefuly ~~on~~ near the water. The wet sand went
between my toes. Sometimes the shells were ~~in~~ on the sand.
Sometimes thay were buried a little. Then I would dig them
up and take off the sand. Found many shells. Aunt Angela
told me their names. Some of them had funny names.
Aunt angela's favorite is a conch shell We love all the
seashells, though. A special kind of treasure!

Go to page 10 in the **Practice** the Strategy ∧ **Notebook!**

Revising

Elaborate

Add interesting details where they are needed.

" I finished my first draft! Now I want to read my paper to my friend Jeremy. I can tell from the **Rubric** that it's important to include details that will interest my readers. I'll ask Jeremy to listen and tell me where I could add more details.

"Jeremy listened as I read. He thought it would be interesting to know the names of some of the shells. Jeremy also asked why Aunt Angela's favorite shell is the conch. I agree with his suggestions. Now I know just what to do! "

[2nd DRAFT]

interesting detail that Isabel added

Found many shells. Aunt Angela told me their names. Some of them had funny names like buttercup, kitten's paw, and lion's paw. Aunt angela's favorite is a conch shell She likes it best becawze she hears the sound of the ocean when she presses it to her ear.

interesting detail that Isabel added

Go to page 12 in the **Practice** the Strategy **Notebook!**

Revising

Clarify
Make sure I used exact words so that my audience can picture everything clearly.

> Did I use exact words? The **Rubric** lets me know that my words are the next thing to check. Exact words will give my audience a clear picture of what I saw and did.
>
> "When I look over my paragraph, I see that I can paint some clearer word pictures with more exact words."

Exact Words

An **exact word** is just the right word to explain what you mean. For example, the word *shark* is more exact than the word *fish*.

[3rd DRAFT]

Aunt Angela took me to a beach on Sanibel Island after a ~~big storm~~ hurricane. It was a great time to hunt for ~~nice~~ unusual shells for my collection. ←*exact word*   *exact word*→

exact word

I ~~walked~~ tiptoed carefuly near the water. The wet sand ~~went~~ oozed between my toes. Sometimes the shells were on the sand. Sometimes thay were buried a little. Then I would dig them up and ~~take~~ brush off the sand.

exact word

Go to page 14 in the **Practice** the Strategy **Notebook!**

Editing

Proofread

Check to see that there are no sentence fragments.

"I've learned from the **Rubric** that conventions and skills are important, so now I will proofread for errors.

"I always check spelling, capitalization, and punctuation. Today, I'll pay special attention to the subjects and predicates in sentences. A sentence needs both a subject and a predicate to be complete. Otherwise, it's only a sentence fragment."

Sentence Fragments

A sentence has a subject and a predicate, and it expresses a complete thought. A **sentence fragment** does not express a complete thought. It is missing either a subject or a predicate.

Fragment: Lived. (Subject is missing.)

Fragment: A tiny hermit crab. (Predicate is missing.)

Sentence: A tiny hermit **crab lived** in the shell. (Both subject and predicate are in this sentence.)

Extra Practice
See **Sentence Fragments** (pages CS 2–CS 3) in the back of this book.

Proofreading Marks

⌐ Indent.

≡ Make a capital.

/ Make a small letter.

∧ Add something.

ℓ Take out something.

⊙ Add a period.

⌗ New paragraph

SP Spelling error

[4th DRAFT]

Going on a Treasure Hunt

Is it a good idea to go to the beach after a storm? It is if you want to find seashells! Aunt Angela took me to a beach on Sanibel Island after a hurricane. It was a great time to hunt for unusual shells for my collection. The wind and waves from the storm made the shells on the ocean floor loose. Then the shells washed up on the beach. I tiptoed carefuly near the water. The wet sand oozed between my toes. Sometimes the shells were on the sand. Sometimes they were buried a little. Then I would dig them up and brush off the sand. Found many shells. Aunt Angela told me their names. Some of them had funny names like buttercup, kitten's paw, and lion's paw. Aunt angela's favorite is a conch shell. She likes it best beeawze she hears the sound of the ocean when she presses it to her ear. We love all the seashells, though. A special kind of treasure!

fragment

fragment

Go to page 15 in the **Practice** the Strategy **Notebook!**

Publishing

Share
Publish my personal narrative paragraph in our class newspaper.

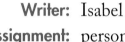

Writer:	Isabel
Assignment:	personal narrative paragraph
Topic:	finding shells on Sanibel Island
Audience:	classmates
Method of Publication:	class newspaper
Reason for Choice:	Some classmates wanted to read about my trip.

> Some friends want to read about my trip to collect shells, so publishing my paragraph in our class newspaper seemed like a good idea. Here's what I did.

1. I copied my paragraph neatly onto a clean sheet of paper.

2. I made sure my final copy had all the changes I made on my drafts.

3. I checked one more time to be sure that there were no errors.

4. I gave my paper to my teacher so that she could put it in the class newspaper.

Going on a Treasure Hunt

by Isabel

Is it a good idea to go to the beach after a storm? It
is if you want to find seashells! Aunt Angela took me to
a beach on Sanibel Island after a hurricane. It was a
great time to hunt for unusual shells for my collection.
The wind and waves from the storm made the shells on
the ocean floor loose. Then the shells washed up on the
beach. I tiptoed carefully near the water. The wet sand
oozed between my toes. Sometimes the shells were on
the sand. Sometimes they were buried a little. Then I
would dig them up and brush off the sand. I found
many shells. Aunt Angela told me their names. Some of
them had funny names like buttercup, kitten's paw, and
lion's paw. Aunt Angela's favorite is a conch shell. She
likes it best because she hears the sound of the ocean
when she presses it to her ear. We love all the seashells,
though. They are a special kind of treasure!

USING the Rubric for Assessment

Go to page 16 in the **Practice ∧ Notebook!** Use that rubric to assess
Isabel's paper. Try using the rubric to assess your own writing.

NARRATIVE

writing

Friendly Letter

Now you are going to learn about another type of narrative writing: a **friendly letter**.

A **friendly letter** is a letter you write to a friend or to someone in your family. It often tells about something that you saw or did.

Read these questions. Then read the friendly letter on the next page. Keep the questions in mind as you read.

 Does the writer tell who the reader of the letter will be? Is the purpose of the letter clear?

 Are the events told in the order in which they happened?

 Does the letter include interesting details?

 Does the letter sound personal? Can you hear the writer's "voice"?

 Are all five letter parts included, written correctly, and punctuated correctly?

heading ——→ 53 Ocean Ave.
Friendship, ME 04547
December 5, 2003

Dear Grandma, ←—— greeting

When we backed out of your driveway, we thought we'd be home soon. Were we wrong! You'll never guess what happened.

At first, we drove along quietly, listening to music. Then Dad suddenly shouted, "Wow!" and stopped the car. I looked up, and there was a huge moose standing in the middle of the road!

Mom thought that maybe the moose would move if we just waited for a while. We waited a few minutes. Then we waited some more. The moose stared at us. We stared at it. That moose just kept standing there.

Finally, Dad turned the car around, and we took the long way home. I don't know why the moose wouldn't move. Maybe it was upset that you hadn't invited it to Thanksgiving dinner, too!

Thank you for inviting all of us, though. It was wonderful to visit with you.

} body

closing ——→ Love,

signature ——→ *Katy*

Using a Rubric

A rubric is a tool that helps you assess a piece of writing. It can also help you figure out if your own writing still needs more work.

How do you use a rubric? You assign 1, 2, 3, or 4 points to tell how well you or another writer did certain things.

Remember the questions you read on page 28? Those questions were used to make this rubric.

"Hi! My name is Justin. I'm learning how to write a friendly letter, too. What did you think of the letter you just read? Look at this rubric. First, read each question. Next, read the scoring information for each question. Then we'll use the rubric to assess the friendly letter."

Audience
Does the writer tell who the reader of the letter will be? Is the purpose of the letter clear?

Organization
Are the events told in the order in which they happened?

Elaboration
Does the letter include interesting details?

Clarification
Does the letter sound personal? Can you hear the writer's "voice"?

Conventions & Skills
Are all five letter parts included, written correctly, and punctuated correctly?

Score 1 Point (Novice)	Score 2 Points (Apprentice)	Score 3 Points (Proficient)	Score 4 Points (Distinguished)
It is very difficult to tell the audience and purpose.	It is somewhat difficult to tell the audience and purpose.	The audience and the purpose are clear.	It is very clear who the reader of the letter will be and why the letter was written.
The events are not in order.	Some of the events are in order.	Most of the events are in order.	All events are told in the order in which they happened.
The letter does not have interesting details.	Only a few interesting details are included.	Some interesting details are included.	A lot of interesting details are included.
There is little evidence of the writer's voice. It is not personal.	There is some evidence of the writer's voice.	The letter has the writer's voice throughout most of the letter.	The letter sounds as if the writer is speaking throughout.
Most letter parts are missing. There are many capitalization and punctuation errors.	Some letter parts are missing. There are some capitalization and punctuation errors.	Most of the letter parts are included. There are few capitalization and punctuation errors.	All of the letter parts appear. Capitalization and punctuation are correct.

Using a **Rubric** to Study the Model

Discuss each question on the rubric with your classmates. Find words and sentences in the friendly letter that help you answer each one. Use the rubric to give Katy's letter a score for each question.

Audience

Does the writer tell who the reader of the letter will be? Is the purpose of the letter clear?

" Yes, I know from the greeting who will receive the letter. "

Dear Grandma,

" The writer is clear about why she is writing the letter. She wants to tell her grandmother what happened on the way home. She also wants to say thank you. "

When we backed out of your driveway, we thought we'd be home soon. Were we wrong! You'll never guess what happened.

Thank you for inviting all of us, though.

Are the events told in the order in which they happened?

❝ Yes, the writer tells the events in a logical order. She uses order words like **first** and **then** to help make the order clear. ❞

At first, we drove along quietly, listening to music. Then Dad suddenly shouted, "Wow!" and stopped the car.

Elaboration

Does the letter include interesting details?

❝ Yes, the writer includes details that will interest her grandma. She would really like the part about the moose. Read what she wrote. ❞

The moose stared at us. We stared at it. That moose just kept standing there.

Clarification

Does the letter sound personal? Can you hear the writer's "voice"?

"I think Katy's letter sounds very personal. Especially near the end, I can really hear Katy's voice. She's got a sense of humor. She made a joke about the moose."

I don't know why the moose wouldn't move. Maybe it was upset that you hadn't invited it to Thanksgiving dinner, too!

Conventions & SKILLS

Are all five letter parts included, written correctly, and punctuated correctly?

"Yes, Katy included all five parts of a friendly letter: the heading, the greeting, the body, the closing, and the signature. She used capital letters and commas correctly in all the parts."

Now it's my turn to write!

I'm going to write my own friendly letter. Follow along to see how I use good writing strategies. I will use the model and the rubric, too.

Justin

Writer of a Friendly Letter

Name: Justin
Home: rural Vermont
Hobbies: hiking, snow tubing, playing chess
Favorite Food: pizza
Assignment: friendly letter

Prewriting

Gather

Decide who my audience will be and why I am writing. Jot notes about my experience.

" In winter, it's usually cold and snowy here in Vermont. I have a cousin, though, who's never even seen snow! Nick, my cousin, lives in California.

"My teacher asked us to write a friendly letter. I decided I'd like to write to my cousin Nick. I want to tell him what happened after a blizzard we just had. I think I'll begin by making a list of the things I did. Nick is my audience. I'll be sure to write what he wants to know. I know that making a list is a good prewriting strategy. "

My Notes on the Blizzard

❄ went snow tubing

❄ built a snow doghouse

❄ made snow people

❄ built a snow fort

Audience

The **audience** is the person or people who will read or hear what you write. Think about what your audience will want to know. Keep your audience in mind all during the writing process.

Go to page 18 in the **Practice Notebook!** the Strategy

Prewriting

Organize
Use my notes to make a sequence chain.

> I know from the **Rubric** that organization is important. Telling things in the order in which they happened will make it easier for Nick to understand what I have written.
>
> "I'll make a sequence chain to help me organize the details from my list. I'll use the chain when I draft my letter. That way I'll be sure to tell the events in order when I write."

Sequence Chain

A **sequence chain** shows steps or events in the order in which they happen.

The Blizzard

First Event	built a snow fort
Next Event	made snow people
Next Event	went snow tubing
Final Event	built a snow doghouse

Go to page 20 in the **Practice** the Strategy **Notebook!**

Write

Draft my friendly letter. Be sure I include all five letter parts.

" Now that I've organized my ideas, I'm ready to write! I know from the model and from the **Rubric** that a friendly letter has five parts. I'll include all those parts when I write my draft.

"I'll look at my sequence chain as I write to be sure that I put the details in order. I won't worry about mistakes in grammar or spelling right now. I can check for those later. "

Parts of a Friendly Letter

- The **heading** tells the address of the person who wrote the letter and the date the letter was written.

- The **greeting** tells who will receive the letter. The greeting begins with *Dear* and ends with a comma after the person's name.

- The **body** is the main part of the letter. It is the writer's message.

- The **closing** ends the letter. The first word begins with a capital letter. The closing ends with a comma. Some examples of closings include: *Your friend, Yours truly, Your pal, Thanks.*

- The **signature** tells who wrote the letter.

heading { 85 Seneca road
Quechee VT 05059
February 15, 2003

Dear Nick ←——— greeting

You know how you're always wishing that you could see real snow? Well, you should have been here last week We had a blizzard that lasted to days!

Our scool was closed for a week, so Matt and I had plenty of time to ~~hang out~~ play in the snow. First, we built a fort. Next, We made ~~a bunch of~~ four snow people in the backyard. They looked great!

After eating pizza for lunch, we decided to go snow tubing on the big hill behind our house. We went really fast. It was a lot of fun! Finally, we built a snow doghouse for Icicle.

I wish that you could have been hear with us. Maybe next year you can visit during school vacation.

body

closing ——→ Your Cousin,

signature ——→ *Justin*

Go to page 21 in the **Practice** the Strategy **Notebook!**

Revising

Elaborate
Add details that will be especially interesting to my audience.

> My first draft is done! Now I can see if I want to make any changes. I know from the **Rubric** that it's important to include details that will interest my reader. I'm going to think about whether Nick will want more details.
>
> "I have an idea! I think Nick would like to know more about what the snow fort and the snow people looked like."

[2nd DRAFT]

interesting detail

Our scool was closed for a week, so Matt and I had plenty of time to play in the snow. First, we built a fort with high walls and a tower. Next, We made four snow people in the backyard. They looked great when we dressed them up with hats and scarves!

interesting detail

Go to page 22 in the **Practice the Strategy Notebook!**

Narrative Writing • Friendly Letter

Revising

Clarify
Make sure my letter has my voice and sounds like me.

"Does my letter sound personal? That's the next thing I'll check. I want to be sure that my letter sounds as if I am speaking to Nick. If my letter doesn't have my own voice, it will sound boring!

"As I go over my letter, I see that I can tell more about what I thought and felt."

READ TO MYSELF

Voice

Writing that has a **voice** lets the reader hear how the writer thinks and feels. Just as a spoken voice "sounds like" the speaker, the writer's voice should "sound like" the writer.

[3rd DRAFT]

After eating pizza for lunch, we decided to go snow tubing on the big hill behind our house. We went ~~really~~ so fast that I was a little scared. It was a lot of fun! Finally, we built a snow doghouse for Icicle. I don't think she liked it very much. I guess it was too chilly in there!

Justin's voice

Go to page 24 in the **Practice** the Strategy **Notebook!**

Editing

Proofread

Check to see that I've used capital letters and commas correctly.

" Now I need to check for errors. I know from the **Rubric** that conventions and skills are important. Today, I'll pay special attention to using capital letters and commas correctly in every part of my letter. "

Capital Letters and Commas in a Friendly Letter

Heading
- Capitalize the name of the street.
- Capitalize abbreviations like *St.* and *Ave.*
- Capitalize the name of the city.
- Use a comma between the city and the state.
- Use two capital letters for the state abbreviation.
- Capitalize the name of the month.
- Use a comma between the day and the year in the date.

Greeting
- Capitalize all the words in the greeting.
- Use a comma after the greeting.

Closing and Signature
- Capitalize the first word of the closing.
- Use a comma after the closing.
- Capitalize your signature.

Extra Practice
See **Punctuating Friendly Letters** (pages CS 4–CS 5) in the back of this book.

Proofreading Marks

⊐ Indent.	Take out something.
≡ Make a capital.	⊙ Add a period.
/ Make a small letter.	# New paragraph
∧ Add something.	(SP) Spelling error

[4th DRAFT]

85 Seneca road

Quechee VT 05059

February 15, 2003

capitals and commas in heading

comma in greeting

Dear Nick

You know how you're always wishing that you could see real snow? Well, you should have been here last week We had a blizzard that lasted to two (sp) days!

Our scool (sp) h was closed for a week, so Matt and I had plenty of time to play in the snow. First, we built a fort with high walls and a tower. Next, We made four snow people in the backyard. They looked great when we dressed them up with hats and scarves!

After eating pizza for lunch, we decided to go snow tubing on the big hill behind our house. We went so fast that I was a little scared. It was a lot of fun! Finally, we built a snow doghouse for Icicle. I don't think she liked it very much. I guess it was too chilly in there!

I wish that you could have been hear here (sp) with us. Maybe next year you can visit during school vacation.

Your Cousin,

comma in closing

capitals in signature → Justin

Go to page 25 in the Practice the Strategy Notebook!

Publishing

Share Mail my letter to my cousin.

Writer:	Justin
Assignment:	friendly letter
Topic:	the big blizzard
Audience:	Nick (Justin's cousin)
Method of Publication:	mail to Nick
Reason for Choice:	Nick likes to hear about snow.

> My letter is almost ready to send to my cousin Nick. Here's what I need to do next.

1. Copy the letter neatly onto a clean sheet of paper. Be sure the final copy includes all the changes I made.

2. Address an envelope. Write the main address and the return address.

3. Fold the letter carefully, and put it in the envelope.

4. Put a stamp on the envelope, and mail the letter.

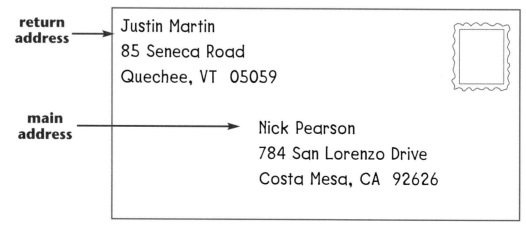

return address →

Justin Martin
85 Seneca Road
Quechee, VT 05059

main address →

Nick Pearson
784 San Lorenzo Drive
Costa Mesa, CA 92626

85 Seneca Road

Quechee, VT 05059

February 15, 2003

Dear Nick,

You know how you're always wishing that you could see real snow? Well, you should have been here last week. We had a blizzard that lasted two days!

Our school was closed for a week, so Matt and I had plenty of time to play in the snow. First, we built a fort with high walls and a tower. Next, we made four snow people in the backyard. They looked great when we dressed them up with hats and scarves!

After eating pizza for lunch, we decided to go snow tubing on the big hill behind our house. We went so fast that I was a little scared. It was a lot of fun! Finally, we built a snow doghouse for Icicle. I don't think she liked it very much. I guess it was too chilly in there!

I wish that you could have been here with us. Maybe next year you can visit during school vacation.

Your cousin,

Justin

USING the Rubric for Assessment

Go to page 26 in the **Practice the Strategy Notebook!** Use that rubric to assess Justin's letter. Try using the rubric to assess your own writing.

your own NARRATIVE writing

Responding to Literature

Put the strategies you practiced in this unit to work to write your own personal narrative, friendly letter or both! You can:

- develop the writing you did in the Your Own Writing pages of the *Practice the Strategy Notebook*;
- pick an idea below and write something new;
- choose another idea of your own.

Be sure to follow the steps in the writing process. Use the rubrics in this unit to assess your writing.

Personal Narrative	**Friendly Letter**
• about a time you were in a play • about a writing or drawing contest you entered • about a time you gave a speech	• to a friend about a book, a movie, or a TV program you liked • to a relative about your favorite author • to a favorite author

portfolio

School–Home Connection

Keep a writing portfolio. Think about adding the activities from the *Practice the Strategy Notebook* to your writing portfolio. You may want to take your portfolio home to share.

DESCRIPTIVE

writing

paints a picture with words.

1

Descriptive Paragraph

2

Descriptive Essay

DESCRIPTIVE writing

Descriptive Paragraph

In this chapter, you will work with one kind of descriptive writing: a **descriptive paragraph**.

A **descriptive paragraph** describes a person, place, or thing. A writer will often use the five senses in a descriptive paragraph. That means a writer will tell about how the topic looks, sounds, feels, tastes, or smells.

Read the questions below. Then read the descriptive paragraph on the next page. Keep the questions in mind as you read.

 Is there an interesting topic sentence that tells the reader the main idea of the paragraph?

 Does the writer use as many of the five senses as she can to tell about the object? Is the information in logical order?

 Does the paragraph use exact adjectives to tell about the topic?

 Does every sentence tell about the main idea?

 Does every sentence begin with a capital letter and end with the correct punctuation mark?

LADY LIBERTY

by Mabel Kwan

The Statue of Liberty in New York Harbor is an amazing sight. The huge statue of a woman stands for freedom. Her mighty right arm stretches 42 feet toward the sky. Her right hand holds a glowing golden torch. On the woman's head is a crown with seven sharp points. The points stand for the world's seven seas and seven continents. The woman's face looks serious and calm. In her left hand, she holds a flat tablet. A date in Roman numerals is written on the tablet: July 4, 1776. The woman wears a long Roman gown with many graceful folds. At her feet is a broken chain, which stands for the freedom the United States won from England. The base of the statue sits inside the walls of an old fort. The fort is covered with rough granite. Did you know that it is more than 305 feet from the base to the tip of the torch? That makes the Statue of Liberty one of the largest statues in the world.

Using a Rubric

A rubric is a tool that helps you assess a piece of writing. It can also help you figure out if your own writing still needs more work.

How do you use a rubric? You assign 1, 2, 3, or 4 points to tell how well you or another writer did certain things.

Remember the questions you read on page 48? Those questions were used to make this rubric.

"Hi! My name is Ramon. I'm learning how to write a descriptive paragraph, too. What did you think of the descriptive paragraph you just read? Look at this rubric. First, read each question. Next, read the information for each question. Then we'll use the rubric to assess the descriptive paragraph."

Audience

Is there an interesting topic sentence that tells the reader the main idea of the paragraph?

Organization

Does the writer use as many of the five senses as she can to tell about the object? Is the information in logical order?

Elaboration

Does the paragraph use exact adjectives to tell about the topic?

Clarification

Does every sentence tell about the main idea?

Conventions & Skills

Does every sentence begin with a capital letter and end with the correct punctuation mark?

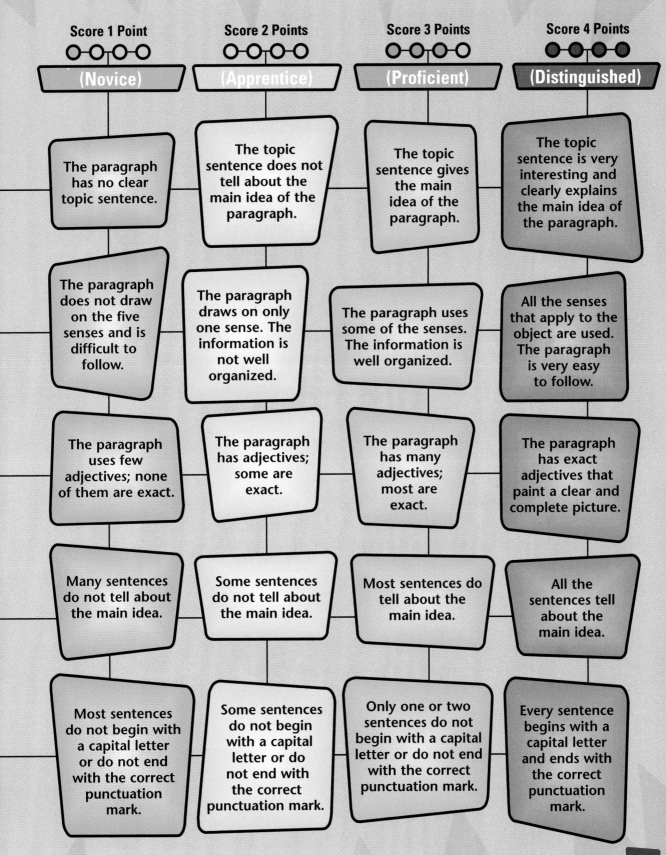

Score 1 Point
(Novice)

The paragraph has no clear topic sentence.

The paragraph does not draw on the five senses and is difficult to follow.

The paragraph uses few adjectives; none of them are exact.

Many sentences do not tell about the main idea.

Most sentences do not begin with a capital letter or do not end with the correct punctuation mark.

Score 2 Points
(Apprentice)

The topic sentence does not tell about the main idea of the paragraph.

The paragraph draws on only one sense. The information is not well organized.

The paragraph has adjectives; some are exact.

Some sentences do not tell about the main idea.

Some sentences do not begin with a capital letter or do not end with the correct punctuation mark.

Score 3 Points
(Proficient)

The topic sentence gives the main idea of the paragraph.

The paragraph uses some of the senses. The information is well organized.

The paragraph has many adjectives; most are exact.

Most sentences do tell about the main idea.

Only one or two sentences do not begin with a capital letter or do not end with the correct punctuation mark.

Score 4 Points
(Distinguished)

The topic sentence is very interesting and clearly explains the main idea of the paragraph.

All the senses that apply to the object are used. The paragraph is very easy to follow.

The paragraph has exact adjectives that paint a clear and complete picture.

All the sentences tell about the main idea.

Every sentence begins with a capital letter and ends with the correct punctuation mark.

Using a Rubric
to Study the Model

Discuss each question in the rubric with your classmates. Find words and sentences in Mabel Kwan's descriptive paragraph that help you answer each one. Use the rubric to assess her paragraph for each question.

Is there an interesting topic sentence that tells the reader the main idea of the paragraph?

" The first sentence names the topic and tells what the paragraph will be about. The topic is the Statue of Liberty, and the main idea is what the statue looks like. The writer says that the statue 'is an amazing sight.' That interested me. It made me want to read more! "

The Statue of Liberty in New York Harbor is an amazing sight.

Does the writer use as many of the five senses as she can to tell about the object? Is the information in logical order?

" The writer uses words like **seven sharp points, a flat tablet,** and **rough granite**. Those words explain how the statue looks and how it might feel to the touch. Her description of Lady Liberty's gown helps me 'see' it. "

The woman wears a long Roman gown with many graceful folds.

" The writer didn't say anything about how the statue smelled or tasted. I guess there might not be much of a smell or taste to a statue. The writer does arrange the information in a logical order. She describes how the statue looks from top to bottom. "

Does the paragraph use exact adjectives to tell about the topic?

" Yes, the paragraph has many colorful details. For example, the writer wrote **glowing golden torch** instead of **beautiful torch**. **Golden** and **glowing** are more colorful words than **beautiful**. They help me picture just what the torch looks like. "

Her right hand holds a glowing golden torch.

Clarification

Does every sentence tell about the main idea?

" Yes, all the sentences describe the Statue of Liberty. There is no unnecessary information. Here is just one example of a good detail sentence. "

In her left hand, she holds a flat tablet. A date in Roman numerals is written on the tablet: July 4, 1776.

Conventions & Skills

Does every sentence begin with a capital letter and end with the correct punctuation mark?

Yes, every sentence begins with a capital letter and ends with the correct punctuation mark. Here are two examples.

Did you know that it is more than 305 feet from the base to the tip of the torch? That makes the Statue of Liberty one of the largest statues in the world.

" ## Now it's my turn to write!

I'm going to write my own descriptive paragraph. I will use the model and the rubric to help me. Follow along to see how I use good writing strategies, too. "

Ramon

Writer of a Descriptive Paragraph

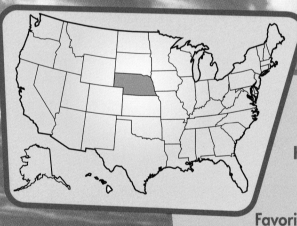

Name: Ramon

Home: Nebraska

Hobbies: building tree houses, computer games, horseback riding

Favorite Book: *Rugby & Rosie* by Nan Parson Rossiter

Favorite Sport: soccer

Assignment: descriptive paragraph

Prewriting

Gather

Make a list of interesting things I have seen. Choose one to write about.

> My teacher asked us to write a paragraph that describes something we've seen. My first step is to choose a topic. I'll start by making a list. I've seen some great things near my home here in Nebraska. I'll also think about things I've seen on trips and on television.

Interesting Things I Have Seen

- baby elephant
- covered wagon
- redwood tree
- high waterfall
- solar-powered car
- huge pumpkin

> I read the ideas on my list and picked one. I would like to write about a redwood tree I saw on a trip to California. One of my hobbies is building tree houses. I can't believe that redwoods can grow so tall! Most of my classmates have never seen a redwood tree. I think they would like to hear a description of one.

Go to page 28 in the **Practice** the Strategy **Notebook!**

Prewriting

Organize

Use what I know about my topic to make an observation chart.

> I know from the **Rubric** that my paragraph needs to have information about how my topic looks, sounds, feels, tastes, or smells. I didn't taste the tree, but I used my other senses. I can record my observations of the redwood tree on a chart. The chart will help me organize my ideas.

Observation Chart

An **observation chart** organizes information. The information is gathered by using the five senses: sight, sound, touch, taste, and smell.

My Topic: Redwood Tree				
Sight	**Sound**	**Touch**	**Taste**	**Smell**
almost 400 feet high	soft rustling sound	bumpy		fresh
wide trunk		rough		clean
grooves in bark		jagged		cedar chest
reddish-brown trunk				
gleaming needles				

Go to page 30 in the **Practice** the Strategy **Notebook!**

Drafting

Write

Draft my paragraph. Make sure it has an interesting topic sentence that tells the main idea.

" My observation chart is finished. I'm ready to write my first draft. I know from the **Rubric** that I need an interesting topic sentence that explains what my paragraph will be about. I'll write that sentence first. "

Topic Sentence

The **topic sentence** tells the reader the main idea of a paragraph. The topic sentence is often the first sentence in the paragraph.

" Next, I'll use my observation chart to help me write the rest of my paragraph. My chart will remind me of which details about the redwood tree to include. I'll do my best with grammar and spelling. I'll fix my errors later. "

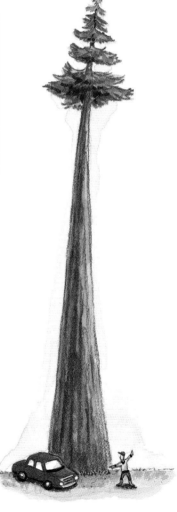

A Very Old Friend

Ramon's topic sentence

Last summer I met a real wooden giant in California. My giant isn't a person. it is the tallest living thing in the world. Can you guess what the giant is. It is ~~really~~ a huge redwood tree that is almost four hundred feet high I stood beside its wide trunk. Its thik bark had many deep grooves. It felt bumpy. Bending my head back, I looked up at the big tree. The reddish-brown trunk seemed ~~like~~ to go on forever The treetop was so far away that it seemed to touch the skye. There were no clouds in the sky that day. The tree was covered with many needles that gleamed in the sunlight. they ~~sounded like~~ made a soft rustling sound as the wind blew through them. I took a depe breath. I liked the fresh smell of the needles. They reminded me of my grandma's old cedar chest. I really don't like the smell of mothballs. my new giant friend isn't just very tall. He is very old, too. In fact, I learned that I would have smelled that same smell if I had stood there two thousand years ago!

Go to page 32 in the **Practice** the Strategy **Notebook!**

Revising

Elaborate — Look for places to use exact adjectives.

" Now I want to improve my paragraph! I know from the **Rubric** that it's important to use exact adjectives. Exact adjectives help paint word pictures.

"When I check my paper, I see that I should add exact adjectives about the tree. Words like **big** and **many** don't really say much to my reader. How can I replace the words to say what I really saw? "

[2nd DRAFT]

Bending my head back, I looked up at the ~~big~~ tall, straight tree.

← exact adjectives

exact adjectives → tiny green

The tree was covered with ~~many~~ tiny green needles that gleamed in the sunlight.

Go to page 34 in the **Practice** the Strategy **Notebook!**

Descriptive Writing • Descriptive Paragraph

Revising

Clarify
Take out details that don't tell about the topic.

READ TO MYSELF

" As I read my paragraph to myself, I think about an important question. Do all the sentences tell about the main idea given in my topic sentence? The **Rubric** helps me know I should check that next.

"When I reread my description, I see that two sentences don't tell about the giant redwood I saw. They don't fit. I'll take them out. "

[3rd DRAFT]

Sentence doesn't tell about the tree.

The treetop was so far away that it seemed to touch the skye. There were no clouds in the sky that day. The tree was covered with tiny green needles that gleamed in the sunlight.

I took a depe breath. I liked the fresh smell of the needles. They reminded me of my grandma's old cedar chest. I really don't like the smell of mothballs. my new giant friend isn't just very tall.

Sentence doesn't tell about the tree.

Go to page 36 in the **Practice** the Strategy **Notebook!**

Editing

Proofread
Check that every sentence begins with a capital letter and ends with the correct punctuation mark.

> I always check spelling, capitalization, and punctuation. I know from the **Rubric** that I should pay special attention to the way each sentence begins and ends. If my sentences don't begin and end correctly, my paragraph will be confusing and hard to read.

Writing Sentences Correctly

- All sentences begin with a **capital letter**.

- A **telling sentence** makes a statement. It ends with a **period**.
  That is an oak tree.

- An **asking sentence** asks a question. It ends with a **question mark**.
  How long did the forest fire last?

- Some sentences give a **command**. Those sentences usually end with a **period**.
  Don't cut down that apple tree.

- Other sentences express **strong feelings**. Those sentences end with an **exclamation point**.
  Wow, that is an old tree!

Extra Practice
See **Writing Sentences Correctly** (pages CS 6–CS 7) in the back of this book.

Proofreading Marks

⌐ Indent.
≡ Make a capital.
/ Make a small letter.
∧ Add something.

ℓ Take out something.
⊙ Add a period.
⌗ New paragraph
SP Spelling error

[4th DRAFT]

A Very Old Friend

Last summer I met a real giant in California. My giant isn't a person. it is the tallest living thing in the world. *— Sentence begins with a capital letter.* Can you guess what the giant is ? *— correct end punctuation* It is a huge redwood tree that is almost four hundred feet high ! I stood beside its wide trunk. Its thik bark *(c SP)* had many deep grooves. It felt bumpy. Bending my head back, I looked up at the tall, straight tree. The reddish-brown trunk seemed to go on forever ! *— correct end punctuation* The treetop was so far away that it seemed to touch the skye. *(sky SP)* The tree was covered with tiny green needles that gleamed in the sunlight. they made a soft *Sentence begins with a capital letter. — ≡* rustling sound as the wind blew through them. I took a depe *(deep SP)* breath. I liked the fresh smell of the needles. They reminded me of my grandma's old cedar chest. my new *Sentence begins with a capital letter. — ≡* giant friend isn't just very tall. He is very old, too. In fact, I learned that I would have smelled that same smell if I had stood there two thousand years ago!

Go to page 37 in the **Practice** ∧ **Notebook!** *(the Strategy)*

Publishing

Share
Read my descriptive paragraph aloud to my class.

Writer:	Ramon
Assignment:	descriptive paragraph
Topic:	a redwood tree
Audience:	classmates
Method of Publication:	reading aloud
Reason for Choice:	The whole class will be able to hear my description.

"Because so many of my friends were interested in my description, I wanted to read it to the whole class. That way everyone would hear about the amazing redwood tree. This is what I did to get my paragraph ready."

1. I made a neat final copy of my paragraph.

2. I made sure my final copy had all the changes I made on my drafts.

3. I practiced reading my paragraph out loud in front of a mirror. I made sure my voice was strong and clear.

4. I brought in some photos of the redwood tree to show the class after I finished reading.

A Very Old Friend
by Ramon

Last summer I met a real giant in California. My giant isn't a person. It is the tallest living thing in the world. Can you guess what the giant is? It is a huge redwood tree that is almost four hundred feet high! I stood beside its wide trunk. Its thick bark had many deep grooves. It felt bumpy. Bending my head back, I looked up at the tall, straight tree. The reddish-brown trunk seemed to go on forever! The treetop was so far away that it seemed to touch the sky. The tree was covered with tiny green needles that gleamed in the sunlight. They made a soft rustling sound as the wind blew through them. I took a deep breath. I liked the fresh smell of the needles. They reminded me of my grandma's old cedar chest.

My new giant friend isn't just very tall. He is very old, too. In fact, I learned that I would have smelled that same smell if I had stood there two thousand years ago!

USING the Rubric for Assessment

Go to page 38 in the **Practice** the Strategy **Notebook!** Use that rubric to assess Ramon's paper. Try using the rubric to assess your own writing.

DESCRIPTIVE writing

Descriptive Essay

In this chapter, you are going to learn about another kind of descriptive writing: a **descriptive essay**.

Like a descriptive paragraph, a **descriptive essay** describes a person, place, or thing. It has several paragraphs that tell how something looks, sounds, feels, tastes, or smells.

Read the questions below. Then read the descriptive essay on the next page. Keep the questions in mind as you read.

 Does the writer's description clearly put the reader in the place being described?

 Does each paragraph have a topic sentence to tell the reader what the paragraph is about? Do detail sentences tell about the topic sentence?

 How well does the writer use comparisons to add to the description?

 Have short, choppy sentences been combined?

 Are the parts of compound sentences correctly joined with a comma and a joining word such as *and, but,* or *or*?

On Top of the World

by Lee Taylor

Some people do not like to go to work. I go to work, and it feels wonderful. In fact, I am on top of the world! That's because I am a construction worker who helps build skyscrapers.

What I enjoy most is the amazing view. I am like a bird sitting in a steel treetop. I see tiny people hurry along crowded sidewalks. Little cars and trucks move slowly down streets that look like a huge game board. Beautiful parks are bright green islands in a sea of cement. Huge ships look like small twigs that float in and out of the harbor. Sometimes, the whole city is wrapped in rays of pink sunlight.

I also like hearing the sounds of the city. Honking horns, jack-hammers, and train whistles join together to play a city song. The sound of the rushing wind is part of the city's music, too.

Other things I enjoy are the feel and the smell of the air high above the ground. I might feel warm, soft breezes. I might have to brace myself against strong gusts of wind. Sometimes damp fog rolls in from the ocean, and I smell salty sea air. What a refreshing smell that is!

I am very lucky to have my job. Many people know the city from the ground up, but not many know it from the top down!

Using a Rubric

A rubric is a tool that helps you assess a piece of writing. It can also help you figure out if your own writing still needs more work.

How do you use a rubric? You assign 1, 2, 3, or 4 points to tell how well you or another writer did certain things.

Remember the questions you read on page 66? Those questions were used to make this rubric.

> Hi! My name is Damara. I'm learning how to write a descriptive essay, too. What did you think of the essay you just read? Look at this rubric. First, read each question. Next, read the information for each question. Then we'll use the rubric to check Lee Taylor's essay.

Audience

Does the writer's description clearly put the reader in the place being described?

Organization

Does each paragraph have a topic sentence to tell the reader what the paragraph is about? Do detail sentences tell about the topic sentence?

Elaboration

How well does the writer use comparisons to add to the description?

Clarification

Have short, choppy sentences been combined?

Conventions & Skills

Are the parts of compound sentences correctly joined with a comma and a joining word such as *and, but,* or *or?*

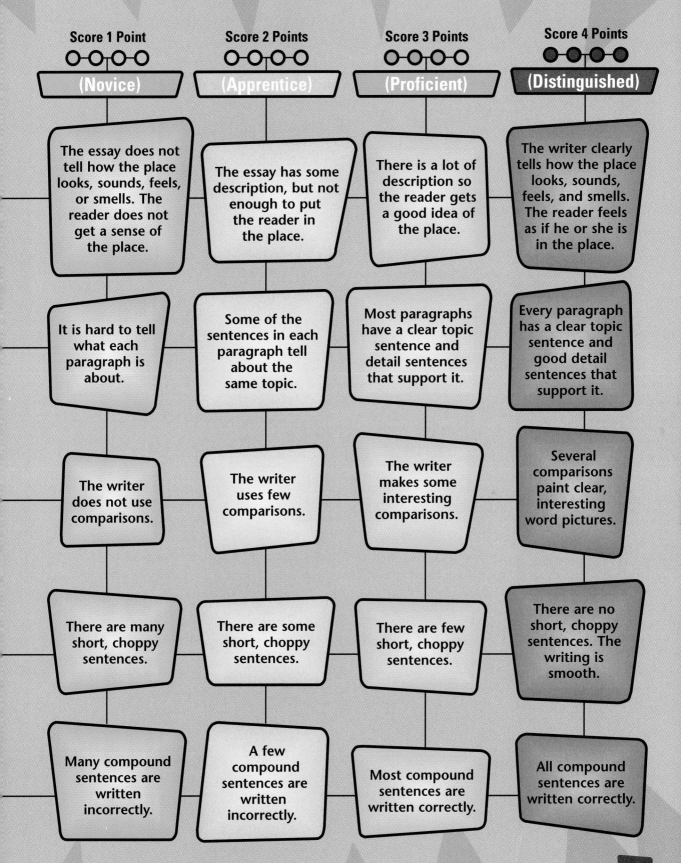

Score 1 Point
(Novice)

The essay does not tell how the place looks, sounds, feels, or smells. The reader does not get a sense of the place.

It is hard to tell what each paragraph is about.

The writer does not use comparisons.

There are many short, choppy sentences.

Many compound sentences are written incorrectly.

Score 2 Points
(Apprentice)

The essay has some description, but not enough to put the reader in the place.

Some of the sentences in each paragraph tell about the same topic.

The writer uses few comparisons.

There are some short, choppy sentences.

A few compound sentences are written incorrectly.

Score 3 Points
(Proficient)

There is a lot of description so the reader gets a good idea of the place.

Most paragraphs have a clear topic sentence and detail sentences that support it.

The writer makes some interesting comparisons.

There are few short, choppy sentences.

Most compound sentences are written correctly.

Score 4 Points
(Distinguished)

The writer clearly tells how the place looks, sounds, feels, and smells. The reader feels as if he or she is in the place.

Every paragraph has a clear topic sentence and good detail sentences that support it.

Several comparisons paint clear, interesting word pictures.

There are no short, choppy sentences. The writing is smooth.

All compound sentences are written correctly.

Using a Rubric
to Study the Model

Discuss each question in the rubric with your classmates. Find sentences in Lee Taylor's essay that help you answer each one.

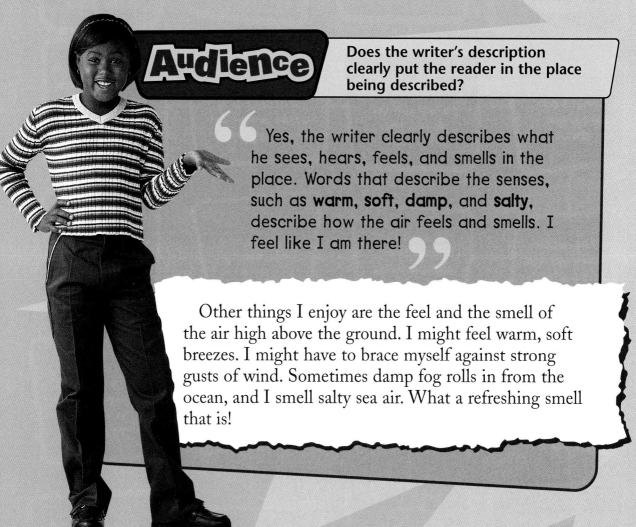

Audience

Does the writer's description clearly put the reader in the place being described?

" Yes, the writer clearly describes what he sees, hears, feels, and smells in the place. Words that describe the senses, such as **warm**, **soft**, **damp**, and **salty**, describe how the air feels and smells. I feel like I am there! "

Other things I enjoy are the feel and the smell of the air high above the ground. I might feel warm, soft breezes. I might have to brace myself against strong gusts of wind. Sometimes damp fog rolls in from the ocean, and I smell salty sea air. What a refreshing smell that is!

Organization

Does each paragraph have a topic sentence to tell the reader what the paragraph is about? Do detail sentences tell about the topic sentence?

" Yes, the first sentence of each paragraph is a topic sentence. It tells me what the paragraph is about. The other sentences give details about the topic sentence.

"For example, I know from the topic sentence that the third paragraph will be about the sounds of the city. The detail sentences explain the topic sentence by describing what the writer hears. "

I also like hearing the sounds of the city. Honking horns, jackhammers, and train whistles join together to play a city song. The sound of the rushing wind is part of the city's music, too.

Elaboration

How well does the writer use comparisons to add to the description?

" Lee Taylor uses many comparisons to help the reader understand. For example, he compares himself to a bird, the streets to a huge game board, and the parks to green islands.

I am like a bird sitting in a steel treetop. I see tiny people hurry along crowded sidewalks. Little cars and trucks move slowly down streets that look like a huge game board. Beautiful parks are bright green islands in a sea of cement.

" Making comparisons helps the writer describe to the reader what he or she sees, hears, feels, and smells. "

Clarification

Have short, choppy sentences been combined?

Yes, short, choppy sentences have been combined. For example, one sentence in the second paragraph could have been four short, choppy sentences: **I see people. They are tiny. They hurry along. The sidewalks are crowded.** "Instead the author has written one smooth sentence.

I see tiny people hurry along crowded sidewalks.

Conventions & Skills

Are the parts of compound sentences correctly joined with a comma and a joining word such as *and, but*, or *or*?

Yes, every compound sentence is written with a comma before the word **and, but,** or **or**.

I go to work, and it feels wonderful.

Many people know the city from the ground up, but not many know it from the top down!

Now it's my turn to write!

I'm going to write my own descriptive essay. Follow along to see how I use the model and the rubric to practice good writing strategies.

DaMaRa

Writer of a Descriptive Essay

Name: Damara

Home: Idaho

Hobbies: canoeing, dancing, drawing

Favorite Book: *Two Days in May* by Harriet Peck Taylor

Favorite Vacation: visiting Yellowstone National Park

Assignment: descriptive essay

Prewriting

Gather
Jot notes that tell how the place looks, sounds, feels, and smells.

" My family took a trip to Yellowstone National Park. It is a beautiful place not too far from my home. I saw amazing things there.

"When our teacher asked us to write a descriptive essay about a place, I chose Yellowstone as my topic. First, I want to jot down notes about how Yellowstone looks, sounds, feels, and smells. "

Yellowstone National Park

- cool lakes
- bubbling mud pots
- an awful smell
- bellowing moose
- loud waterfalls
- deep canyons
- elk with pointed antlers
- sweet-smelling wildflowers

- roaring geysers
- forests—green and thick
- bears with shiny fur
- foaming rivers
- colorful rock steps
- loud swan
- rolling meadows

Go to page 40 in the **Practice** the Strategy **Notebook!**

Descriptive Writing • Descriptive Essay

Prewriting

Organize

Use my notes to make a spider map.

> I see that the model essay is organized by the senses. The writer of that essay describes what he sees, hears, feels, and smells. I think I will organize my essay by the things I enjoyed most—the scenery, the animals, and the geysers and hot springs. I will use a spider map to organize my notes. I will write my main topic in the circle. Then on each "leg" of the spider I will write **scenery, animals,** and **geysers and hot springs**. On the lines coming from the legs, I will write details.

Spider Map

A **spider map** organizes information about a topic. Write the main topic in the center of the "spider." On the spider's "legs," write topic sentence ideas. Write descriptive details on the lines coming from the "legs." These details should support the topic sentence ideas.

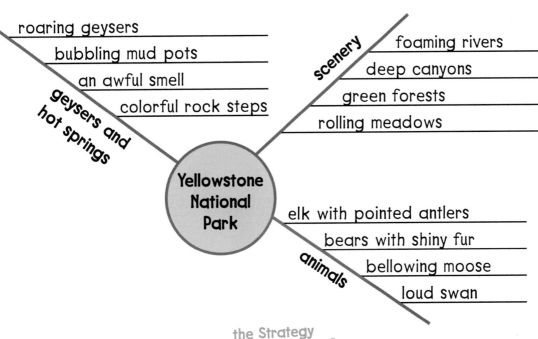

roaring geysers

bubbling mud pots

an awful smell

colorful rock steps

geysers and hot springs

scenery

foaming rivers

deep canyons

green forests

rolling meadows

Yellowstone National Park

elk with pointed antlers

bears with shiny fur

bellowing moose

loud swan

animals

Go to page 42 in the **Practice** the Strategy **Notebook!**

Drafting

Write

Draft my essay. Write a topic sentence for each paragraph. Write detail sentences for every topic sentence.

“ Now I'm ready to draft my essay! First, I'll write a beginning paragraph. Then I'll write three paragraphs, using a leg of my spider map for each one. Finally, I'll write an ending paragraph.

“I know from the **Rubric** that every paragraph should have a topic sentence. That's the sentence that tells the main idea of the paragraph. I also know that each topic sentence needs detail sentences to explain the main idea. Read part of my essay on the next page. Only the last paragraph is missing. ”

Detail Sentences

A **detail sentence** explains the topic sentence. The detail sentences give examples and tell the reader about the main idea of the paragraph.

topic sentence   **My Favorite Place**   [ist DRAFT]

Yellowstone National park is the most wonderful place I

detail sentences

have ever visited. ~~There's~~ It has something amazing arownd

every corner. My favorite things about my favorite place are

the scenery, the animals, and the geysers and hot springs.

The first thing you notice is the beautiful scenery. Foaming   ← topic sentence

detail sentences

rivers ~~are~~ run through canyons. The canyons are deep. Thick

green forests grow near cool lakes and rocky cliffs. There

are rolling meadows. They are covered with sweet-smelling

wildflowers. Huge waterfalls are loud.   topic sentence

Yellowstone is home to many animals. It has elk with long,

detail sentences

pointed antlers. shaggy buffalo roam freely. Bears with shiny

fur somtimes walk right beside the road! If you are lucky, you

will ~~see~~ hear the bellow of a moose or the loud call of a

swan. It is nice to look at the animals don't try to feed them.

They are better off eating the food they find naturally.   topic sentence

The park is also famous for its geysers and hot springs.

detail sentences

Roaring geysers send boiling water shooting high into the air

Some hot springs are bubbling mud pots. They look really

cool they smell awful! Other springs have colorful rock steps.

Go to page 44 in the **Practice** the Strategy **Notebook!**

ReVising

Elaborate — Add details that compare one thing to another.

" My first draft is finished, and I like it! Now I'll see if I can make the essay even better.

"I've learned from the **Rubric** that comparing something to something else can make my writing clearer, easier to understand, and more interesting. I could add a comparison to describe how the waterfalls sound. I could also add a comparison to show how the mud pots look and smell. "

Comparisons

A **comparison** takes two different things and shows a way in which they are alike. In this example, the sound of a swan is compared to the sound of a trumpet.

Example: The **swan's call** sounded like a loud note played on a **trumpet**.

[2nd DRAFT]

There are rolling meadows. They are covered with sweet-smelling wildflowers. Huge waterfalls ~~are loud~~.

comparison that Damara added ⟶ sound like thunder

∧ like steaming soup

Some hot springs are bubbling mud pots. They look ∧ ~~really cool~~ like rotten eggs! ← **comparisons that Damara added** ∧

they smell ~~awful~~ Other springs have colorful rock steps.

∧

Go to page 46 in the **Practice** the Strategy **Notebook!**

Descriptive Writing • Descriptive Essay

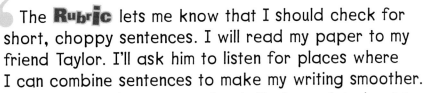

Revising

Clarify Combine short, choppy sentences.

"The **Rubric** lets me know that I should check for short, choppy sentences. I will read my paper to my friend Taylor. I'll ask him to listen for places where I can combine sentences to make my writing smoother.

"After I read my essay aloud, Taylor pointed out two places where I could combine short, choppy sentences. I like his ideas!"

READ TO A PARTNER

Short, Choppy Sentences

Two **short, choppy sentences** can be joined if they express one idea. Here are two short, choppy sentences.

We swam in a pond. The pond was shallow.

Here is one way to join the two short, choppy sentences into one sentence.

We swam in a shallow pond.

This sentence is easier to read.

[3rd DRAFT]

The first thing you notice is the beautiful scenery. Foaming rivers
deep ←—**combine short, choppy sentences**
run through ^canyons. ~~The canyons are deep.~~ Thick green forests

grow near cool lakes and rocky cliffs. ~~There are rolling meadows.~~
Rolling meadows ←—**combine short, choppy sentences**—↗
~~They~~ ^are covered with sweet-smelling wildflowers. Huge waterfalls

sound like thunder.

Go to page 48 in the **Practice** the Strategy **Notebook!**

Descriptive Writing • Descriptive Essay

Editing

Proofread

Check that the main parts of each compound sentence are joined with a comma and a joining word.

"I always check spelling, capitalization, and punctuation. Today I'll pay special attention to compound sentences. I'll be sure each one has a comma and a joining word."

Conventions & Skills

Compound Sentences

A **compound sentence** is made of two sentences connected by a joining word such as *and, but,* or *or.* A comma goes before the conjunction. A conjunction is a joining word.

Two Sentences: The bears look cute. They can be dangerous.
Compound Sentence: The bears look cute, **but** they can be dangerous.

Extra Practice
See **Compound Sentences** (pages CS 8–CS 9) in the back of this book.

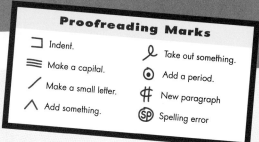

[4th DRAFT]

My Favorite Place

Yellowstone National park is the most wonderful place I have
ever visited. It has something amazing around every corner. My
favorite things about my favorite place are the scenery, the
animals, and the geysers and hot springs.

Yellowstone is home to many animals. It has elk with long,
pointed antlers. shaggy buffalo roam freely. Bears with shiny fur
sometimes walk right beside the road! If you are lucky, you will
hear the bellow of a moose or the loud call of a swan. It is nice
to look at the animals , but don't try to feed them. ← *compound sentence* They are better
off eating the food they find naturally.

The park is also famous for its geysers and hot springs. Roaring
geysers send boiling water shooting high into the air. Some hot
springs are bubbling mud pots. , but ← *compound sentence* They look like steaming soup they
smell like rotten eggs! Other springs have colorful rock steps.

Yellowstone National Park has interesting scenery, animals, and
geysers and hot springs. Yellowstone National Park is my favorite
place , and I cant wait to go there again. ← *compound sentence* Nowhere else in the world is
like it!

Go to page 49 in the **Practice** the Strategy **Notebook!**

Publishing

Share
Post my description on the bulletin board.

Writer:	Damara
Assignment:	descriptive essay
Topic:	Yellowstone National Park
Audience:	classmates
Method of Publication:	bulletin board
Reason for Choice:	My classmates can read and learn about Yellowstone National Park.

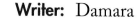

" I was ready to publish my essay! I liked the idea of putting it on the class bulletin board. My friends could read it whenever they wanted. Here's what I did. "

1. I made a neat final copy of my essay.
2. I checked one more time to be sure there were no errors.
3. I got a large piece of colorful construction paper that was larger than my essay.
4. I tacked the colored paper to the bulletin board. Then I tacked my essay and drawing to the center of the colored paper.

Descriptive Writing • Descriptive Essay

My Favorite Place
by Damara

Yellowstone National Park is the most wonderful place I have ever visited. It has something amazing around every corner. My favorite things about my favorite place are the scenery, the animals, and the geysers and hot springs.

The first thing you notice is the beautiful scenery. Foaming rivers run through deep canyons. Thick green forests grow near cool lakes and rocky cliffs. Rolling meadows are covered with sweet-smelling wildflowers. Huge waterfalls sound like thunder.

Yellowstone is home to many animals. It has elk with long, pointed antlers. Shaggy buffalo roam freely. Bears with shiny fur sometimes walk right beside the road! If you are lucky, you will hear the bellow of a moose or the loud call of a swan. It is nice to look at the animals, but don't try to feed them. They are better off eating the food they find naturally.

The park is also famous for its geysers and hot springs. Roaring geysers send boiling water shooting high into the air. Some hot springs are bubbling mud pots. They look like steaming soup, but they smell like rotten eggs! Other springs have colorful rock steps.

Yellowstone National Park has interesting scenery, animals, and geysers and hot springs. Yellowstone National Park is my favorite place, and I can't wait to go there again. Nowhere else in the world is like it!

USING the Rubric for Assessment

Go to page 50 in the **Practice** the Strategy **Notebook!** Use that rubric to assess Damara's paper. Try using the rubric to assess your own writing.

your own DESCRIPTIVE writing

Science

Put the strategies you practiced in this unit to work to write your own descriptive paragraph, descriptive essay, or both! You can:

- develop the writing you did in the Your Own Writing pages of the *Practice the Strategy Notebook*;

- pick an idea below and write something new;

- choose another idea of your own.

Be sure to follow the steps in the writing process. Use the rubrics in this unit to assess your writing.

Descriptive Paragraph (a thing)	Descriptive Essay
• a plant or a flower • an unusual machine • a science experiment • a fruit or a vegetable • an unusual animal	• at a science museum or a science fair • on a hill or a mountain • at a beach or a lake • in a park or on a nature trail

portfolio

School–Home Connection

Keep a writing portfolio. Think about adding the activities from the *Practice the Strategy Notebook* to your writing portfolio. You may want to take your portfolio home to share.

EXPOSITORY

writing

explains something or gives facts.

1

How-To Essay

2

Factual Report

writing

How-To Essay

In this chapter, you will work with one kind of expository writing: a **how-to essay**.

A **how-to essay** explains how to do something or how to make something. It tells the steps in order. It also tells the reader what materials are needed.

Read the questions below. Then read the how-to essay on the next page. Keep the questions in mind as you read.

 Does the essay tell the reader exactly what materials are needed to complete the project?

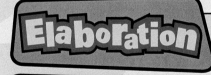 Are the how-to steps told in order?

 Is every step given? Is the information for each step complete?

 Do time-order words make the order of the steps clear?

 When choosing homophones, does the writer use the correct one?

The Perfect Sandwich

by Oscar Cooper

Does your stomach ever scream, "I'm hungry"? Then you'll want to learn how to make the best peanut butter sandwich ever. Not only does it taste great, but it's good for you, too!

First, gather all the ingredients. You'll need two slices of bread, a big glob of peanut butter, a banana, several raisins, strawberry jam, and some granola. Put them on your kitchen counter.

Next, spread the peanut butter on one side of a slice of bread. Be sure that the peanut butter covers the whole surface of the bread evenly. There shouldn't be any lumps.

Now, use the banana, raisins, jam, and granola to make a face on the peanut butter. Cut three round banana slices. Use two for the eyes and one for the nose. Place the raisins side by side in a curve to form a smiling mouth. Then drop a dab of strawberry jam on either side of the nose to make rosy cheeks. Add some crunchy freckles by sprinkling a little granola over the face.

Finally, it's time to enjoy your creation! Take a minute to admire the smiling face. Smile back as you think about how happy your stomach is going to be. Put the second piece of bread on top of the first. You're about to taste the best sandwich ever made!

Using a
Rubric

A rubric is a tool that helps you check a piece of writing. It can also help you figure out if your own writing still needs more work.

How do you use a rubric? You assign 1, 2, 3, or 4 points to tell how well you or another writer did certain things.

Remember the questions you read on page 86? Those questions were used to make this rubric.

" Hi! My name is Meg. I'm learning to write a how-to essay, too. What did you think of the essay you just read? Look at this rubric. First, read each question. Next, read the scoring information for each question. Then we'll use the rubric to assess the how-to essay. **"**

Audience

Does the essay tell the reader exactly what materials are needed to complete the project?

Organization

Are the how-to steps told in order?

Elaboration

Is every step given? Is the information for each step complete?

Clarification

Do time-order words make the order of the steps clear?

When choosing homophones, does the writer use the correct one?

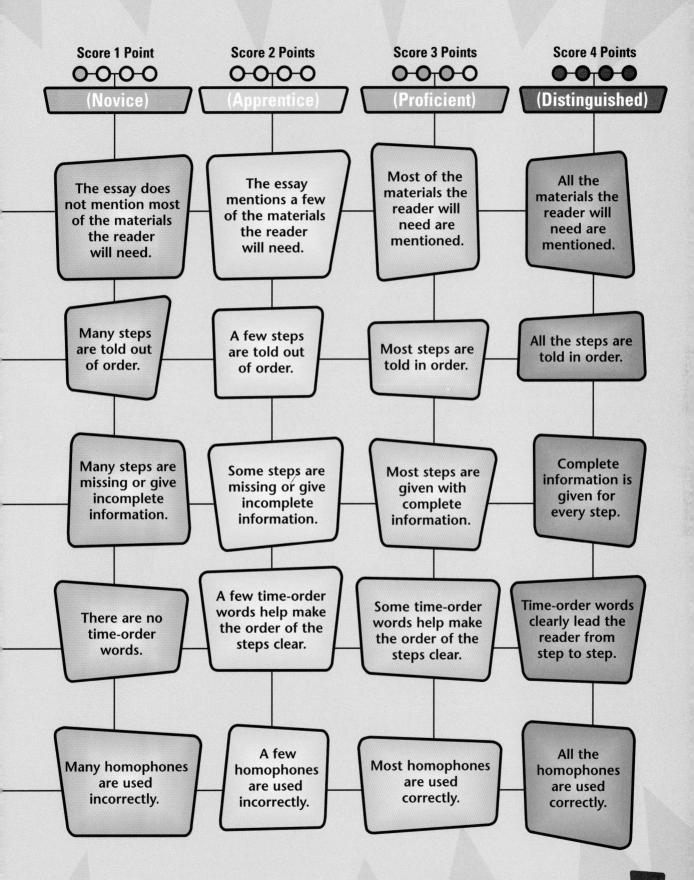

Score 1 Point

(Novice)

The essay does not mention most of the materials the reader will need.

Many steps are told out of order.

Many steps are missing or give incomplete information.

There are no time-order words.

Many homophones are used incorrectly.

Score 2 Points

(Apprentice)

The essay mentions a few of the materials the reader will need.

A few steps are told out of order.

Some steps are missing or give incomplete information.

A few time-order words help make the order of the steps clear.

A few homophones are used incorrectly.

Score 3 Points

(Proficient)

Most of the materials the reader will need are mentioned.

Most steps are told in order.

Most steps are given with complete information.

Some time-order words help make the order of the steps clear.

Most homophones are used correctly.

Score 4 Points

(Distinguished)

All the materials the reader will need are mentioned.

All the steps are told in order.

Complete information is given for every step.

Time-order words clearly lead the reader from step to step.

All the homophones are used correctly.

Using a Rubric

to Study the Model

Discuss each question on the rubric with your classmates. Find words and sentences in Oscar Cooper's essay that help you answer each one. Use the rubric to assess the essay.

 **Audience**

Does the essay tell the reader exactly what materials are needed to complete the project?

" Yes, in the second paragraph the writer names all the ingredients the reader needs to make the sandwich. Read what he wrote. "

First, gather all the ingredients. You'll need two slices of bread, a big glob of peanut butter, a banana, several raisins, strawberry jam, and some granola. Put them on your kitchen counter.

Organization Are the how-to steps told in order?

" Yes, the steps are all in order. Read how the writer explains the second step. "

Next, spread the peanut butter on one side of a slice of bread. Be sure that the peanut butter covers the whole surface of the bread evenly. There shouldn't be any lumps.

Elaboration Is every step given? Is the information for each step complete?

" The writer remembered to give every step, and he gave complete information for each one. For example, the writer tells exactly what to do to make the face. "

Now, use the banana, raisins, jam, and granola to make a face on the peanut butter. Cut three round banana slices. Use two for the eyes and one for the nose. Place the raisins side by side in a curve to form a smiling mouth. Then drop a dab of strawberry jam on either side of the nose to make rosy cheeks. Add some crunchy freckles by sprinkling a little granola over the face.

Clarification

Do time-order words make the order of the steps clear?

66 Yes, time-order words, such as **first, next, now,** and **finally,** clearly lead the reader from step to step. Here are some examples. 99

First, gather all the ingredients.

Next, spread the peanut butter on one side of a slice of bread.

Conventions & SKILLS

When choosing homophones, does the writer use the correct one?

66 Homophones, such as **its** and **it's** and **your** and **you're,** sound the same, but they have different spellings and meanings. Look at the paragraph below. In the first sentence, the writer chose **it's,** not **its,** because it stands for **it is.** The writer always chose the correct homophone. 99

Finally, *it's* time to enjoy *your* creation! Take a minute to admire the smiling face. Smile back as you think about how happy *your* stomach is going to be. Put the second piece of bread on top of the first. *You're* about to taste the best sandwich ever made!

66 ## Now it's my turn to write!

I'm going to write my own how-to essay. Follow along to see how I practice using good writing strategies and the rubric, too. 99

MEG

Writer of... How-To Essay

How-To Essay

Name: Meg
Home: Michigan
Hobbies: camping, skiing, writing stories
Favorite Author: Beverly Cleary
Assignment: how-to essay

Prewriting

Gather

Make a list of everything the reader will need to do the project.

" My teacher wanted everyone to write a how-to essay. He asked what we know how to do. He asked what we are good at making. We discovered we are all experts at something!

"I thought about how much I like to go camping. I've set up a tent many, many times. I know exactly how to do it. I decided to write down the instructions so that others could learn how to do it, too!

"My first step is to make a list of all the things someone would need to do this project. "

Materials for Setting Up a Tent

- sheet of plastic
- a tent
- tent poles
- tent stakes
- a hammer or a rock

Go to page 52 in the **Practice the Strategy Notebook!**

Expository Writing • How-To Essay

Prewriting

Organize
Use the items in my list to make a sequence chain.

> I know from the **Rubric** that I need to tell the how-to steps in order. If the steps aren't in order, my readers will be confused. They won't be able to set up the tent!
>
> "Before I start writing, I will organize my ideas in a sequence chain. I'll use the list of materials I just made to help me think of the order of the steps.

Sequence Chain

A **sequence chain** shows steps in the order in which they should happen.

Setting Up a Tent
Step 1 Decide where to put the tent and get ground ready.
Step 2 Lay plastic sheet and tent on the ground.
Step 3 Attach poles and raise the tent.
Step 4 Fold in edges of the plastic sheet.
Step 5 Pound in stakes to keep the tent from moving.

Go to page 54 in the **Practice** the Strategy **Notebook!**

Drafting

Write

Draft my essay by separating the steps in the sequence chain into paragraphs.

"" I've organized my ideas. Now I can draft my how-to essay. First, I'll write a beginning paragraph. It will tell what my how-to essay is about. Then I'll write the how-to paragraphs.

"When I studied the **Rubric**, I learned that the how-to steps should be told in order. I can make sure they are by writing one paragraph for each step I listed in my sequence chain. I'll be sure my readers are clear about each step. ""

Paragraph

A **paragraph** is a group of sentences that have the same topic or purpose. The sentences focus on a single main idea or thought. The first sentence of a paragraph starts on a new line and is indented.

Building My Tent in the Woods

[ist DRAFT]

beginning paragraph

If you like being outdoors and camping, then you'll want to learn to set up a tent It's really easy to do!

Step 1

First, you need to find a good spot for your tent. ~~The~~ Choose a place where the ground is levul. It should not be hilly or rocky.

Step 2

Put down a sheet of plastic. Smooth it out ~~and~~ with your hands so that their are no rinkles. Spread out the tent on top of the plastic.

Step 3

Now it's time to attach the poles. First, take them out of they're bag. Unfold each one, and snap the ends of the sections into place. Next, slide each pole into it's sleeve on the tent. The ends ~~should~~ of the poles will stick out. To raise the tent, lift each pole and place the end into a metal ring ~~near~~ on the floor of the tent.

Step 4

Next, fold in the edges of the plastic. If the plastic hangs out, it could make rainwater run under the tent!

Step 5

Finally, pull out the big loops at the bottom edges of the tent. Put a tent stake in each loop. Use a hammer or a rock to pound the stakes into the ground. Now your tent won't move, and your ready to spend a great night in the woods!

Go to page 56 in the **Practice** the Strategy **Notebook!**

Revising

Elaborate
Add information to fill in gaps in my how-to essay.

> I think I did a good job on my first draft, but I'm not finished working on my essay yet. I know from the **Rubric** that I should check to make sure that I've given every step. I also need to make sure that the information for each step is complete. I want to read my paper to myself to be sure that nothing is missing.
>
> "When I read my how-to essay, I discovered that I forgot to talk about clearing the tent site. That's a gap I should fill in now!"

[2nd DRAFT]

First, you need to find a good spot for your tent. Choose a place where the ground is levul. It should not be hilly or rocky. Then pick up everything that might make lumps under your tent, like stones or twigs.

← *information that Meg added*

Go to page 58 in the **Practice** the Strategy **Notebook!**

Revising

Clarify
Use time-order words to make the order of the steps clear.

66 I can tell from the **Rubric** that time-order words are important in a how-to essay. Did I use them to lead readers from step to step?

"As I checked my essay, I saw two places where I could add time-order words to make the order of the steps clearer. 99

Time-Order Words

Time-order words are signal words that tell the order in which steps or events happen.

Time-Order Words Include:

first	next	today
second	then	yesterday
third	last	tomorrow

[3rd DRAFT]

Second, Put down a sheet of plastic. Smooth it out with your
← **time order words** →
hands so that their are no rinkles. Then Spread out the tent on

top of the plastic.

Go to page 60 in the **Practice** the Strategy **Notebook!**

Editing

Proofread
Check that each homophone fits its meaning.

> Mistakes in my essay might confuse my readers, so my last strategy is to proofread for errors.
>
> "I always check spelling, capitalization, and punctuation. The **Rubric** reminds me to pay special attention to the homophones. Now I'll make sure I've used every homophone correctly."

Homophones

Homophones are words that sound the same but have different spellings and meanings.

	Meaning	**Example**
its	belonging to it	I love **its** smoky flavor.
it's	it is	Now **it's** my turn to cook.
their	belonging to them	We used **their** tent.
there	in or at that place	Put the logs over **there**.
they're	they are	**They're** hiking today.
your	belonging to you	Is that **your** sleeping bag?
you're	you are	Tell us when **you're** leaving.

Extra Practice
See **Homophones**
(pages CS 10–CS 11) in the back of this book.

Expository Writing • How-To Essay

[4th DRAFT]

Building My Tent in the Woods

If you like being outdoors and camping, then you'll want to learn to set up a tent⊙ It's really easy to do!

First, you need to find a good spot for your tent. Choose a place where the ground is ~~levul~~ level (SP). It should not be hilly or rocky. Then pick up everything that might make lumps under your tent, like stones or twigs.

Second, ∧Put down a sheet of plastic. Smooth it out with your hands so that ~~their~~ there ← corrected homophone are no ~~rinkles~~ wrinkles (SP). Then ~~Spread~~ spread out the tent on top of the plastic.

Now it's time to attach the poles. First, take them out of their ← corrected homophone ~~they're~~ bag. Unfold each one, and snap the ends of the sections into place. Next, slide each pole into ~~it's~~ its ← corrected homophone sleeve on the tent. The ends of the poles will stick out. To raise the tent, lift each pole and place the end into a metal ring on the floor of the tent.

Next, fold in the edges of the plastic. If the plastic hangs out, it could make rainwater run under the tent!

Finally, pull out the big loops at the bottom edges of the tent. Put a tent stake in each loop. Use a hammer or a rock to pound the stakes into the ground. Now your tent won't move, and ~~your~~ you're ← corrected homophone ready to spend a great night in the woods!

Go to page 61 in the **Practice** ∧the Strategy **Notebook!**

Publishing

Share
Publish my essay in a class book of how-to essays.

Writer: Meg
Assignment: how-to essay
Topic: setting up a tent
Audience: classmates and other students
Method of Publication: class book of how-to essays
Reason for Choice: My teacher asked everyone to write an essay for the book.

" I really liked the idea of publishing my essay in a class book of how-to essays. The book will go into the school library. That way lots of students can read the essays. We learned in making the book that we are all good at doing or making something! I can't wait to read the other essays. We can all learn how to do and make many new things! Here are the steps I followed. "

1. First, I made a neat final copy of my essay.

2. Then I made sure my final copy had all the changes that I made on my drafts.

3. Next, I checked one more time to be sure that there were no errors.

4. Finally, I glued my essay to a sheet of colored paper and gave it to my teacher.

Building My Tent in the Woods

by Meg

If you like being outdoors and camping, then you'll want to learn to set up a tent. It's really easy to do!

First, you need to find a good spot for your tent. Choose a place where the ground is level. It should not be hilly or rocky. Then pick up everything that might make lumps under your tent, like stones or twigs.

Second, put down a sheet of plastic. Smooth it out with your hands so that there are no wrinkles. Then spread out the tent on top of the plastic.

Now it's time to attach the poles. First, take them out of their bag. Unfold each one, and snap the ends of the sections into place. Next, slide each pole into its sleeve on the tent. The ends of the poles will stick out. To raise the tent, lift each pole and place the end into a metal ring on the floor of the tent.

Next, fold in the edges of the plastic. If the plastic hangs out, it could make rainwater run under the tent!

Finally, pull out the big loops at the bottom edges of the tent. Put a tent stake in each loop. Use a hammer or a rock to pound the stakes into the ground. Now your tent won't move, and you're ready to spend a great night in the woods!

USING the Rubric for Assessment

Go to page 62 in the **Practice ∧ Notebook!** Use that rubric to assess
the Strategy
Meg's paper. Try using the rubric to assess your own writing.

writing

Factual Report

In this chapter, you will learn about another kind of expository writing: a **factual report**.

A **factual report** gives information that is real, not made up. It gives facts about a topic.

Read the questions below. Then read the factual report on the next page. Keep the questions in mind as you read.

Does an interesting introduction make the reader want to read more?

Is the report organized into an introduction, body, and conclusion?

Is there enough information in each body paragraph to support the main idea of the paragraph?

Do all of the facts have something to do with the topic of the report?

Are past-tense verbs formed correctly?

Game Time

by Sally Loz

You might be eight or nine years old, but chances are you've played a game that has been around for thousands of years. What is that game? It's checkers. The game of checkers has a long and surprising history.

It isn't clear exactly where and when checkers was first played. However, a board game similar to checkers was found in the ruins of an ancient city in Iraq. That game is about 5,000 years old! Another early form of checkers was played in Egypt more than 3,000 years ago. The game board is carved into the stone of an ancient Egyptian temple. You can still see it today.

How did checkers spread to other parts of the world? About 1,300 years ago, some people from Africa invaded Spain. They brought their form of checkers with them. The game changed a little when someone, perhaps in the south of France, decided to play it on a chessboard. Then later, in France, the rules changed again. The game became more like our modern game of checkers.

Today, checkers is played all over the world. It has many different names. If you were in England, you would play draughts (pronounced *drafts*). In Italy, you would play darma. Almost anywhere you go, you can play this popular game with a very long history.

Using a **Rubric**

A rubric is a tool that helps you evaluate a piece of writing. It can also help you figure out if your own writing still needs more work.

How do you use a rubric? You assign 1, 2, 3, or 4 points to tell how well you or another writer did certain things.

Remember the questions you read on page 104? Those questions were used to make this rubric.

> **❝** Hi! My name is Al. I'm learning how to write a factual report, too. What did you think of the report you just read? Look at this rubric. First, read each question. Next, read the scoring information for each question. Then we'll use the rubric to decide how well the writer did. **❞**

Audience

Does an interesting introduction make the reader want to read more?

Organization

Is the report organized into an introduction, body, and conclusion?

Elaboration

Is there enough information in each body paragraph to support the main idea of the paragraph?

Clarification

Do all of the facts have something to do with the topic of the report?

Conventions & Skills

Are past-tense verbs formed correctly?

Score 1 Point	Score 2 Points	Score 3 Points	Score 4 Points
(Novice)	**(Apprentice)**	**(Proficient)**	**(Distinguished)**
The report has no clear introduction.	The report has an introduction, but it is probably not interesting to most readers.	The introduction is somewhat interesting to most readers.	An excellent introduction would make nearly all readers want to read more.
The report does not have a clear introduction, body, or conclusion.	The report has one clear part—for example, an introduction—but other parts are not clear.	The report has two clear parts—for example, an introduction and a conclusion—but the body is not clear.	The report has a clear introduction, body, and conclusion.
Much important information is missing in the body paragraphs.	Some important information is missing in the body paragraphs.	Most of the important information is given in the body paragraphs.	All the important information is given.
Many facts in the report do not have anything to do with the topic.	Some facts given have something to do with the topic.	Most of the facts given have something to do with the topic.	All of the facts in the report have something to do with the topic.
Most past-tense verbs are not formed correctly.	Some past-tense verbs are formed correctly.	Most past-tense verbs are formed correctly.	All past-tense verbs are formed correctly.

Using a Rubric
to Study the Model

Discuss each question on the rubric with your classmates. Find words and sentences in the factual report that help you answer each one. Use the rubric to decide how well Sally Loz did on her report.

Audience

Does an interesting introduction make the reader want to read more?

" Yes, the first sentence of the introduction really grabbed my attention. What game do I play that is thousands of years old? I wanted to keep reading! The introduction also made the topic of the report clear. "

You might be eight or nine years old, but chances are you've played a game that has been around for thousands of years. What is that game? It's checkers. The game of checkers has a long and surprising history.

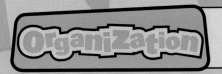

Is the report organized into an introduction, body, and conclusion?

" Yes. We already read how Sally introduced her topic. She also has two body paragraphs that support the topic. "The first body paragraph tells about when and where the game started. The second body paragraph tells how the game spread to different parts of the world. "

Another early form of checkers was played in Egypt more than 3,000 years ago.

About 1,300 years ago, some people from Africa invaded Spain. They brought their form of checkers with them.

" The conclusion restates the fact that the game has a long history. "

Almost anywhere you go, you can play this popular game with a very long history.

Is there enough information in each body paragraph to support the main idea of the paragraph?

" Yes, there is enough information in each body paragraph to support the main idea. The writer's information is complete. "

It isn't clear exactly where and when checkers was first played. However, a board game similar to checkers was found in the ruins of an ancient city in Iraq. That game is about 5,000 years old!

" Yes, the writer gives explanations about the history of the game and gives examples of where it spread in the world. The information in the conclusion, for example, gives more facts about the name the game has in different parts of the world. "

Today, checkers is played all over the world. It has many different names. If you were in England, you would play draughts (pronounced *drafts*). In Italy, you would play darma. Almost anywhere you go, you can play this popular game with a very long history.

Conventions & SKILLS

Are past-tense verbs formed correctly?

" Yes, past-tense verbs are always formed correctly. In these two sentences, the writer uses the correct past-tense form of the verbs **bring (brought)**, **change (changed)**, and **decide (decided)**. "

They brought their form of checkers with them. The game changed a little when someone, perhaps in the south of France, decided to play it on a chessboard.

" Now it's my turn to write!

I'm going to write my own factual report. I will use the rubric and the model. Follow along to see how I practice using good writing strategies. "

Al

Writer of a Factual Report

Name: Al
Home: North Dakota
Hobbies: snowshoeing, collecting stamps, photography
Favorite Book: *The Mountain That Loved a Bird* by Alice McLerran
Favorite Foods: spaghetti, corn on the cob, oatmeal
Favorite Subject: social studies
Assignment: factual report

Prewriting

Gather

Write two questions to guide my research. Use a book or the Internet. Take notes to answer my questions.

"My assignment is to write a factual report. My teacher asked us to choose a topic that we want to learn more about.

"I really like snowshoeing. My mom told me that Native Americans used snowshoes hundreds of years ago. I want to know more about the history of snowshoes. I'll write two questions I have about them. The questions should be interesting to me and my readers. Then I'll do research on the Internet to find the answers to the questions.

"My teacher helped me look up the Web sites on the computer. She made sure we only went to sites we could trust. I found some Web sites on Native Americans and some on snowshoes. They all helped me with my research. I found lots of facts about snowshoes. "

Question 1: Where and when were snowshoes first used?

Question 2: Have snowshoes changed over the years?

My Notes:

- early snowshoes—made of wood and leather
- snowshoes—first used in Asia 6,000 years ago
- snowshoes—came to America over land bridge from Asia
- new snowshoes—made of metal and cloth
- snowshoes—Native Americans in North America used
- some old snowshoes more than seven feet long

Go to page 64 in the **Practice** the Strategy **Notebook!**

Prewriting

Organize
Use my notes to make a network tree.

" I know from the **Rubric** that my report should be well organized. The topic has to be clear, and each paragraph should tell about only one main idea.

"I can see that I need to make a plan! A network tree will help me organize my ideas. First, I'll write down my questions. Then I'll use my notes to answer each question with facts I found when I searched the Internet. "

Network Tree

A **network tree** organizes information. For a factual report, the topic goes at the top of the tree. Questions about the topic go on the next level. Facts that answer the questions go on the bottom level.

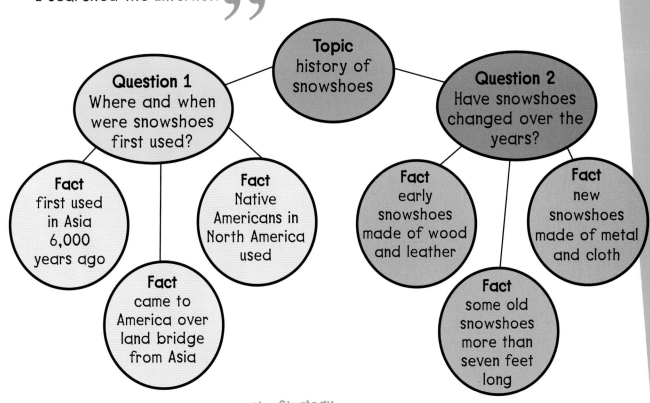

Topic
history of snowshoes

Question 1
Where and when were snowshoes first used?

Question 2
Have snowshoes changed over the years?

Fact
first used in Asia 6,000 years ago

Fact
came to America over land bridge from Asia

Fact
Native Americans in North America used

Fact
early snowshoes made of wood and leather

Fact
some old snowshoes more than seven feet long

Fact
new snowshoes made of metal and cloth

Go to page 66 in the **Practice the Strategy Notebook!**

Drafting

Write

Write an introduction that states the topic in an interesting way. Write one paragraph for every question on the network tree in the body. Write a conclusion to tie ideas together.

❝ Now I'm ready to draft my report. I know from the **Rubric** that my introduction should make the reader want to keep reading. I should also clearly state the topic of my report.

"After I write my introduction, I can use the questions and answers from my network tree to draft two paragraphs for the body of my report. My first body paragraph will be about my first question. My second body paragraph will be about my second question. The body paragraphs are the main part of the report. Each paragraph should talk about only one main idea of my topic.

"Finally, I'll write a conclusion that ties everything together. The conclusion will bring my report to an end. ❞

Parts of a Report

The **introduction** is the first paragraph of a report. It states the topic of the report. A good introduction also catches the audience's attention.

The **body** is the main part of the report. The body comes between the introduction and the conclusion. The body gives the main ideas of the report. It answers the writer's questions.

The **conclusion** ties up the ideas of the report and restates the topic.

Walking on Snow

introduction

Have you ever tried walking in deep snow? If you have, you know that your feet sink in, and it is hard to move. Long ago, people found a solution to this problum—snowshoes! ← **topic**

body

Answers Question 1.

Many scientists ~~are~~ think that snowshoes were first used about 6,000 years ago in asia. Some scientists believe people brung them to America when they went over a land bridge. That bridge join Asia and Alaska. Native Americans start wearing snowshoes. They made many different kinds of snowshoes for different types of snow.

Answers Question 2.

Snowshoes ~~didn't have~~ change over the years. ~~They~~ The old ones had wood frames and leather webbing. Some were more than seven feet long! Now, modern snowshoes are smaller and lighter. Modern bicycles are also lighter than ones made long ago. Modern snowshoes are usually made of metal and cloth. Most people who use them want to have fun in the snow!

conclusion

Snowshoeing is very popular today. ~~When~~ Modern snowshoes are simple to use. you don't need to learn any fancy footwork. Just strap them on your feet, and do something people did thouzands of years ago!

Go to page 68 in the **Practice** the Strategy **Notebook!**

ReVising

Elaborate
Check that there is enough information in each body paragraph.

> I like my first draft, but I have more work to do. I know from the **Rubric** that I need enough information in the body of my report to support my topic.
>
> "My first body paragraph tells about where and when Native Americans first wore snowshoes. It would be helpful to tell why they wore them, too. I remember from my research that there was a reason the Native Americans started wearing snowshoes. That would be an interesting fact. I will add that to my report."

[2nd DRAFT]

Many scientists think that snowshoes were first used about 6,000 years ago in asia. Some scientists believe people brung them to America when they went over a land bridge.

information that Al added

That bridge join Asia and Alaska. Native Americans start
→ so they could hunt, trap, and move more easily in winter
wearing snowshoes. They made many different kinds of
snowshoes for different types of snow.

Go to page 71 in the **Practice** the Strategy **Notebook!**

Expository Writing • Factual Report

Revising

Clarify

Check that all the facts have something to do with the topic of the report.

"I know from the **Rubric** that my facts have to clearly support the topic of my report. That means that everything I talk about in this report should be about snowshoes.

READ TO A PARTNER

"My friend Joy listened as I read my report. She noticed a sentence that told a fact that did not have anything to do with snowshoes. I will go back and take that sentence out. I'm glad that Joy is a good listener!"

[3rd DRAFT]

Snowshoes change over the years. The old ones had wood frames and leather webbing. Some were more than seven feet long! Now, modern snowshoes are smaller and lighter. Modern bicycles are also lighter than ones made long ago. ← **fact does not tell about snowshoes**

Go to page 72 in the **Practice** the Strategy **Notebook!**

Editing

Proofread
Check that past-tense verbs are formed correctly.

"I don't want mistakes in my report to confuse my readers, so now I'll proofread for errors.

"I always check spelling, capitalization, and punctuation. The **Rubric** reminds me that today I should pay special attention to past-tense verbs."

Past-Tense Verbs

Past-tense verbs show that the action happened in the past. Many past-tense verbs end in *-ed*.

Present Tense	Past Tense
hope(s)	hoped
use(s)	used

Some verbs do not add *-ed* to make the past tense. They have different forms. These verbs are called **irregular verbs**.

Present Tense	Past Tense
bring(s)	brought
give(s)	gave
go(es)	went
sing(s)	sang
sleep(s)	slept
take(s)	took

Extra Practice
See **Past-Tense Verbs**
(pages CS 12–CS 13) in the back of this book.

[4th DRAFT]

Walking on Snow

Have you ever tried walking in deep snow? If you have, you know that your feet sink in, and it is hard to move. Long ago,
                                                            problem (SP)
people found a solution to this ~~problem~~—snowshoes!

Many scientists think that snowshoes were first used about 6,000
                                              brought ← **correct**
years ago in asia. Some scientists believe people ~~brung~~ them to**past-**
                                                   joined **tense**
America when they went over a land bridge. That bridge ~~join~~   **form**
        correct past-tense form → started
Asia and Alaska. Native Americans ~~start~~ wearing snowshoes so
they could hunt, trap, and move more easily in winter. They made
many different kinds of snowshoes for different types of snow.
              changed ← **correct past-tense form**
Snowshoes ~~change~~ over the years. The old ones had wood
frames and leather webbing. Some were more than seven feet long!
Now, modern snowshoes are smaller and lighter. Modern snowshoes
are usually made of metal and cloth. Most people who use them
want to have fun in the snow!

Snowshoeing is very popular today. Modern snowshoes are
simple to use. you don't need to learn any fancy footwork. Just(SP)
                                                 thousands
strap them on your feet, and do something people did ~~thouzands~~
of years ago!

                                        the Strategy
Go to page 73 in the **Practice** ∧ **Notebook!**

Publishing

Share
Present my report to a small group of my classmates. Answer any questions they have.

Writer: Al

Assignment: factual report

Topic: history of snowshoes

Audience: classmates

Method of Publication: read aloud

Reason for Choice: Several friends can hear the report at one time and discuss it.

" It's time to present my report! I'm glad that I'll be able to read it to a group of my classmates. I know that some of them also like snowshoeing, and I think they'll be interested in the topic. Here's how I got ready! "

1. First, I made a neat final copy of my report.

2. Then I made sure that my final copy had all the changes I'd made on my drafts.

3. Next, I found pictures of old snowshoes and modern snowshoes to go with my report. I decided when I would show each picture.

4. Finally, I practiced reading my report out loud and displaying the pictures. I practiced reading slowly, loudly, and clearly.

Walking on Snow

by Al

Have you ever tried walking in deep snow? If you have, you know that your feet sink in, and it is hard to move. Long ago, people found a solution to this problem—snowshoes!

Many scientists think that snowshoes were first used about 6,000 years ago in Asia. Some scientists believe people brought them to America when they went over a land bridge. That bridge joined Asia and Alaska. Native Americans started wearing snowshoes so they could hunt, trap, and move more easily in winter. They made many different kinds of snowshoes for different types of snow.

Snowshoes changed over the years. The old ones had wood frames and leather webbing. Some were more than seven feet long! Now, modern snowshoes are smaller and lighter. Modern snowshoes are usually made of metal and cloth. Most people who use them want to have fun in the snow!

Snowshoeing is very popular today. Modern snowshoes are simple to use. You don't need to learn any fancy footwork. Just strap them on your feet, and do something people did thousands of years ago!

USING the Rubric for Assessment

Go to page 74 in the **Practice** ∧ **Notebook!** Use that rubric to assess
the Strategy
Al's paper. Try using the rubric to assess your own writing.

your own EXPOSITORY writing
Social Studies

Put the strategies you practiced in this unit to work to write your own how-to essay, factual report, or both! You can:

- develop the writing you did in the Your Own Writing pages of the *Practice the Strategy Notebook*;

- pick an idea below and write something new;

- choose another idea of your own.

Be sure to follow the steps in the writing process. Use the rubrics in this unit to assess your writing.

How-to Essay
• how to make a map • how to be a good citizen • how to prepare a special food from another country • how to start your own business • how to make a time line

Factual Report
• the history of your town or city • an important person from your state or city • a famous place in your town or state • the history of a holiday • the importance of a special tradition or celebration

portfolio

School–Home Connection

Keep a writing portfolio. Think about adding the activities from the *Practice the Strategy Notebook* to your writing portfolio. You may want to take your portfolio home to share.

NARRATIVE

fiction writing

tells a story about characters and events that are made up.

1

Realistic Story

2

Folktale

NARRATIVE

fiction writing

Realistic Story

In this chapter, you will learn about a kind of writing called the **realistic story**.

A **realistic story** tells about people, events, and places that *could* be real but are not real.

The story on the next page is a realistic story. Read these questions. Then read the story. Keep the questions in mind as you read.

 Does the writer choose a topic that is interesting to the readers?

 Is the story easy to follow with a clear beginning, middle, and end?

 Does the story have dialogue to make the characters seem more real?

 Does each sentence lead clearly to the next sentence?

 Are all pronouns in their correct form?

OH, THAT FRED

by Dennis Chow

Fred is the newest member of Jeremy's family. He's a little Welsh terrier with black and tan fur that feels like a stiff paintbrush. Fred is just six months old. A very frisky fellow, he seems to like to play tricks. Some of his tricks are cute, but some of his tricks are not cute at all.

Last week, Fred gave Jeremy and his family a terrible scare. Jeremy called Fred to go for their afternoon walk, but Fred didn't answer. Jeremy kept calling and calling, but Fred never came. Jeremy told his mom, and they started to hunt all over the house for Fred. Suddenly, with a worried look on her face, Mom asked Jeremy, "Could Fred have gotten out of the house somehow?"

At first, Jeremy didn't think that was possible. Then he said fearfully, "Maybe Fred pushed open the screen door. Maybe he even found another way to get out of the house."

Mom and Jeremy didn't lose a minute after that. First, they looked in the backyard. Then they started walking around the neighborhood. They called "Fred!" again and again. They told their neighbors that Fred was missing and asked for help. Soon many people were helping them. All over the neighborhood, people were calling, "Fred! Fred! Fred!"

The search for Fred had been going on for more than an hour when Jeremy got really upset. Jeremy loved his puppy, and Fred was gone! Mom put her arm around his shoulder and said, "Don't worry too much, Jeremy. I have a feeling that we're going to find him." After another hour, though, they went home, and their neighbors stopped looking, too.

Later that afternoon, feeling sad and lonely, Jeremy reached under his bed for his shoes. He felt something furry. He looked under the bed, and there was Fred sound asleep. Maybe the little dog hadn't heard their calls. More likely, he had heard them, but he hadn't bothered to answer them. Jeremy let out a sigh of relief. Oh, that Fred!

Using a Rubric

A rubric is a tool that helps you check a piece of writing. It can also help you figure out if your own writing still needs more work.

How do you use a rubric? You give 1, 2, 3, or 4 points to tell how well you or another writer did certain things.

Remember the questions you read on page 124? Those questions were used to make this rubric.

> " Hi! My name is Lauren. I'm learning how to write a realistic story, too. What did you think of the realistic story you just read? Look at this rubric. First, read each question. Next, read the scoring information for each question. Then we'll use the rubric to assess the realistic story. "

Audience
Does the writer choose a topic that is interesting to the readers?

Organization
Is the story easy to follow with a clear beginning, middle, and end?

Elaboration
Does the story have dialogue to make the characters seem more real?

Clarification
Does each sentence lead clearly to the next sentence?

Conventions & Skills
Are all pronouns in their correct form?

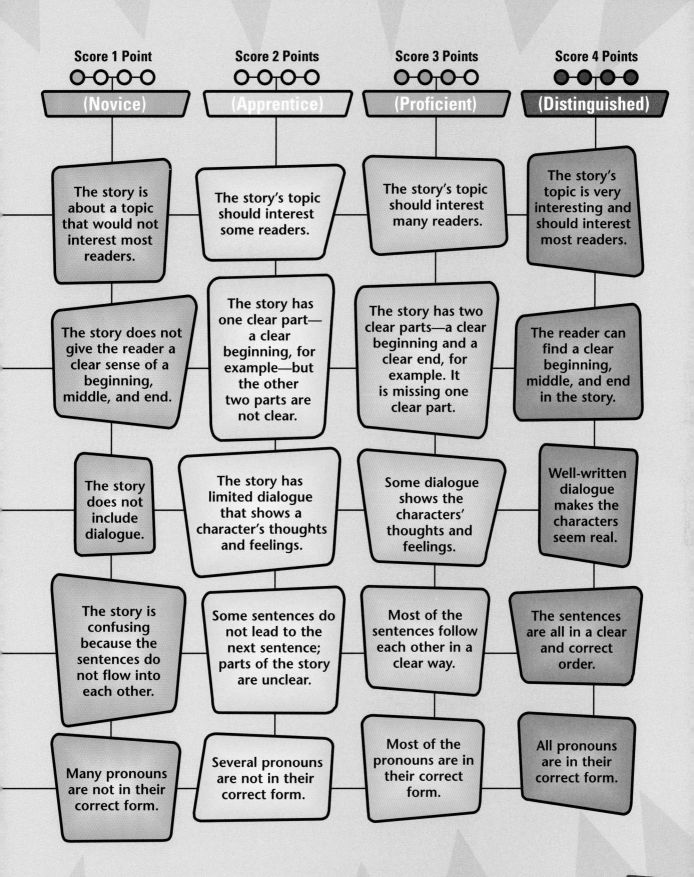

Score 1 Point
(Novice)

The story is about a topic that would not interest most readers.

The story does not give the reader a clear sense of a beginning, middle, and end.

The story does not include dialogue.

The story is confusing because the sentences do not flow into each other.

Many pronouns are not in their correct form.

Score 2 Points
(Apprentice)

The story's topic should interest some readers.

The story has one clear part—a clear beginning, for example—but the other two parts are not clear.

The story has limited dialogue that shows a character's thoughts and feelings.

Some sentences do not lead to the next sentence; parts of the story are unclear.

Several pronouns are not in their correct form.

Score 3 Points
(Proficient)

The story's topic should interest many readers.

The story has two clear parts—a clear beginning and a clear end, for example. It is missing one clear part.

Some dialogue shows the characters' thoughts and feelings.

Most of the sentences follow each other in a clear way.

Most of the pronouns are in their correct form.

Score 4 Points
(Distinguished)

The story's topic is very interesting and should interest most readers.

The reader can find a clear beginning, middle, and end in the story.

Well-written dialogue makes the characters seem real.

The sentences are all in a clear and correct order.

All pronouns are in their correct form.

Using a Rubric to Study the Model

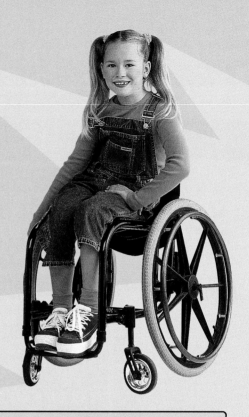

Discuss each question on the rubric with your classmates. Find words and sentences in the realistic story that help you answer each one.

Audience

Does the writer choose a topic that is interesting to the readers?

"Yes. The topic is very interesting. Most of my friends have pets. Fred sounds really cute. I want to read about him. These sentences make me want to read more."

A very frisky fellow, he seems to like to play tricks. Some of his tricks are cute, but some of his tricks are not cute at all.

Is the story easy to follow with a clear beginning, middle, and end?

❝ I think that the beginning, middle, and end of this story are clear. The writer starts by telling the reader about Fred. Fred is the newest member of Jeremy's family. He is a frisky puppy who plays tricks. That's a clear beginning. ❞

Fred is the newest member of Jeremy's family. He's a little Welsh terrier with black and tan fur that feels like a stiff paintbrush. Fred is just six months old. A very frisky fellow, he seems to like to play tricks. Some of his tricks are cute, but some of his tricks are not cute at all.

❝ The middle is clear, too. Fred is lost. The ending is also clear. Fred is found, and Jeremy is very happy. ❞

Elaboration

Does the story have dialogue to make the characters seem more real?

❝ The writer has the characters speak to each other in some places in the story. Their dialogue (what they say to each other) tells what might have happened. It helps show the characters' thoughts and feelings, too. ❞

Suddenly, with a worried look on her face, Mom asked Jeremy, "Could Fred have gotten out of the house somehow?"

At first, Jeremy didn't think that was possible. Then he said fearfully, "Maybe Fred pushed open the screen door. Maybe he even found another way to get out of the house."

Clarification

Does each sentence lead clearly to the next sentence?

> Every sentence leads clearly to the next one. The story flows and makes sense. Look at the way the writer helps us understand how Fred was finally discovered.

Later that afternoon, feeling sad and lonely, Jeremy reached under his bed for his shoes. He felt something furry. He looked under the bed, and there was Fred sound asleep.

Conventions & Skills

Are all pronouns in their correct form?

> Pronouns can be tricky. This writer knows when to use **I**, **we**, **him**, and **they**. Look at this example.

Mom put her arm around his shoulder and said, "Don't worry too much, Jeremy. I have a feeling that we're going to find him." After another hour, though, they went home, and their neighbors stopped looking, too.

> In this sentence, **I** refers to Mom and **we** refers to Mom, Jeremy, and the neighbors. **I** and **we** are subject pronouns since Mom and Jeremy are the subjects of the sentence.

Now it's my turn to write!

I'm going to write my own realistic story. I will use the model and the rubric. Follow along with me to see how I practice good writing strategies, too.

LAUREN

Writer of a Realistic Story

Name: Lauren

Home: Delaware

Favorite Book: *The Great Gilly Hopkins* by Katherine Paterson

Favorite Ways to Make Friends: school, wheelchair basketball, after-school activities

Assignment: realistic story

Prewriting

Gather

Brainstorm story ideas. Choose one. List characters and events. Write an action sentence.

" Everyone in my class is going to write a story. We talked about what our topics could be. My teacher said a good way to start is to brainstorm ideas. We decided to brainstorm things that third grade kids find hard to do. That will be a place to start to come up with a topic for our stories. "

Brainstorm

When people want to come up with ideas they can **brainstorm**. In a brainstorm people say all of the ideas that pop into their heads about a topic or subject. Then they make a list of all of the ideas.

" Here is the list of things that my class came up with. "

Class Brainstorming Ideas:
Things That Third-Grade Students Find Hard to Do

- having to talk in front of the class

- meeting new stepbrothers and stepsisters

- joining a new activity group when you don't know anyone

- going to a new school in a new neighborhood

- eating something from all the food groups

- going to bed on time

Narrative Writing • Realistic Story

" Our teacher had us each choose one topic to write about from our class brainstorming list. I chose to write about a boy going to a new school in a new neighborhood. I think I will name my main character Tony, after my uncle Tony. Since Tony is going to a new school, I'm sure he will be worried about what the other kids will be like. Here is the list I made of events and characters. "

My Brainstorming List

- big move for Tony
- has to go to new school
- many worries
- mother tries to help
- great first day
- students clapping
- Tony happy

" The next thing I have to do is write an action sentence. The action sentence will tell who and what is most important about my story. "

Prewriting

Gather

Brainstorm story ideas. Choose one. List characters and events. Write an action sentence.

" A story has to have action—things that happen. I used my brainstorming list to help me come up with an action sentence. "

Action Sentence

The **action** tells what happens in a story. It doesn't mean a character has to run around. The character can even be *sleeping*. The events in the story are the action.

An **action sentence** tells who does what and how it comes out. For example, in the story *The Three Billy Goats Gruff* the action sentence could be, "Three billy goats outsmart a troll and are able to cross the bridge." The action sentence for the story "Oh, That Fred" could be, "Fred disappears, but he is found under the bed." Writing an action sentence can help you plan your story.

> The action sentence tells who did what in my story. I have already decided the main character from my list of events and characters. His name will be Tony. Now I will tell what he will do.

My Action Sentence

Tony Leva was worried about going to a new school, but the students were friendly.

> **My action sentence tells:**
> **Who:** Tony Leva
> **Does what:** worried about a new school
> **How it comes out:** students are friendly

Go to page 76 in the **Practice** the Strategy **Notebook!**

Prewriting

Organize

Make a storyboard. Write a caption for every picture.

> "A story is made up of things that happen. Those are the events. When I write my story, I have to put the events in order. I know from the **Rubric** that organization is important. My storyboard will show the key events in order. I will make my storyboard go from top to bottom. I'll write a caption for each picture. Each picture and caption will tell what happened to Tony when he went to his school."

Storyboard With Captions

A **storyboard** uses pictures to put story events in order. A storyboard can go from top to bottom or from left to right.

A **caption** tells what is happening in a picture. A caption is usually placed beneath the picture.

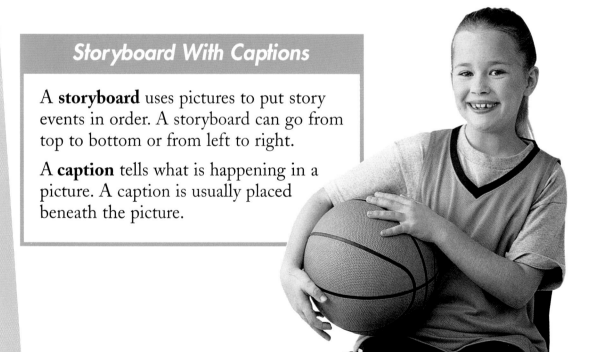

My Storyboard

Event 1

Caption: Tony is so worried that he just sits in his room.

Event 2

Caption: Tony doesn't know anyone in his new school.

Event 3

Caption: Tony smiles as the class claps for him.

Go to page 78 in the **Practice** the Strategy **Notebook!**

Drafting

Write

Draft my story. Make sure that my story has a clear beginning, middle, and end.

"Now I can start writing my story. I know from the **Rubric** that my story should have three parts. I'll use my storyboard to help me.

"First, for my beginning, I'll write about how worried Tony is about going to his new school. That's Event 1 on my storyboard.

"Then, for the middle, I'll write about the beginning of his first day and his first few minutes in the classroom. That's Event 2 on my storyboard.

"Last, for my ending, I'll write about how Tony's feelings change. That's Event 3 on my storyboard. I already have an idea for one of my pictures. I will go ahead and sketch it now.

"I won't worry about mistakes in grammar and spelling now. I can fix those later."

The New Boy in School

beginning

Tony Leva was worried. The next day would be his first day at Jefferson School. Him and his famly had moved in the middle of march. Everyone in the third grade would already know everyone else. Tony was sure that no one would ~~like~~ care about a new student. He was also sure that no one would ~~need~~ want a new friend. In fact, Tony was so worried that he just sat in his room all day.

middle

The next morning, Tony felt worse. His stomach hurt, and his head hurt, too. Him and his mom walked to school. On the way, his mother talked to him. Tony didn't feel any better, though. He walked slowly to his classroom. After his mother left, he felt even worse. Lots of students were talking and laughing in the hallway. He didnt know anybody.

Expecting the worst, Tony walked into Ms. Nozawa's classroom. Everyone stopped working. Everyone looked up at Ms. Nozawa and he. Many of the girls and boys smiled. Suddenly, them all started to clap! Ms. Nozawa clapped, too.

end

Tony was so happy he could not speak, but he smiled at everyone. Maybe, thought Tony, he was going to make freinds at Jefferson School after all.

Go to page 80 in the **Practice** the Strategy **Notebook!**

Revising

Elaborate
Add dialogue to make my characters seem more real.

" I read my first draft to myself. Then I remembered from the **Rubric** that dialogue brings the characters to life.

"I think that Tony's mom should say something helpful. I also want to show Ms. Nozawa being kind, too. If I make my characters speak to each other, they will sound more real. "

Dialogue

In a story, **dialogue** is the talking that goes on between the characters. Put quotation marks before and after a speaker's words in a dialogue sentence.

[2nd DRAFT]

The next morning, Tony felt worse. His stomach hurt, and his head hurt, too. Him and his mom walked to school. On the way, his mother talked to him. She said, "You'll like your new school, Tony." Tony didn't feel any better, though. ← **dialogue**

Expecting the worst, Tony walked into Ms. Nozawa's classroom. Ms. Nozawa saw him right away and exclaimed, "Wonderful! Here's Tony!" ← **dialogue**

Go to page 82 in the **Practice** the Strategy **Notebook!**

Revising

Clarify
Reorder sentences to make sure the story flows well and makes sense.

" I know from the **Rubric** that one sentence should lead clearly to the next. The sentences need to be in an order that flows and makes sense. That will help my writing sound smooth. When I read my paper again, I found two sentences out of order. "

[3rd DRAFT]

The next morning, Tony felt worse. His stomach hurt, and his head hurt, too. Him and his mom walked to school. On the way, his mother talked to him. She said, "You'll like your new school, Tony." Tony didn't feel any better, though. He walked slowly to
reordered sentences
his classroom. After his mother left, he felt even worse. Lots of students were talking and laughing in the hallway. He didnt know anybody.

Go to page 84 in the **Practice** the Strategy **Notebook!**

Editing

Proofread
Check to see that all pronouns are in their correct form.

Now I need to check for errors. I know from the **Rubric** that I should check all the pronouns I've written. After I check my spelling, capitalization, and punctuation, I'm going to make sure that I've used all pronouns correctly.

Pronouns

Pronouns are words that take the place of nouns. Some pronouns are **subject pronouns**. They are subjects of sentences. Other pronouns are **object pronouns**. Object pronouns can go after action verbs. Object pronouns can also go after words such as *at*, *for*, *of*, *to*, and *with*.

Subject Pronouns	Object Pronouns
I, you, he, she, it, we, they	me, you, him, her, it, us, them
Example Sentences:	**Example Sentences:**
I smile at Tony.	Ms. Nozawa greeted **him**.
He smiles back.	Tony smiled at **us**.
We make friends.	

Extra Practice
See **Subject and Object Pronouns**
(pages CS 14–CS 15) in the back of this book.

Tony Leva was worried. The next day would be his first day at

subject pronoun ——→ He

Jefferson School. Him and his famly ⊕ had moved in the middle of

march. Everyone in the third grade would already know everyone

else. Tony was sure that no one would care about a new student.

He was also sure that no one would want a new friend. In fact,

Tony was so worried that he just sat in his room all day.

The next morning, Tony felt worse. His stomach hurt, and his

He ←— subject pronoun

head hurt, too. Him and his mom walked to school. On the way,

his mother talked to him. She said, "You'll like your new school,

Tony." Tony didn't feel any better, though. After his mother left,

he felt even worse. He walked slowly to his classroom. Lots of

students were talking and laughing in the hallway. He didn't

know anybody.

Expecting the worst, Tony walked into Ms. Nozawa's classroom.

Ms. Nozawa saw him right away and exclaimed, "Wonderful! Here's

Tony!" Everyone stopped working. Everyone looked up at Ms.

him ←— object pronoun

Nozawa and he. Many of the girls and boys smiled. Suddenly,

subject ——→ they

pronoun them all started to clap! Ms. Nozawa clapped, too. Then she said,

"Welcome to our class, Tony. Mark will be your partner today.

He will answer all your questions. He will be your pal at recess,

and then he will eat lunch with you, too."

Go to page 85 in the **Practice ⌃ Notebook!**

the Strategy

Publishing

Share

Publish my story as a chapter in a book for my classroom library.

Writer:	Lauren
Assignment:	realistic story
Topic:	going to a new school
Audience:	classmates
Method of Publication:	a chapter for a class book
Reason for Choice:	I want my classmates to read this story.

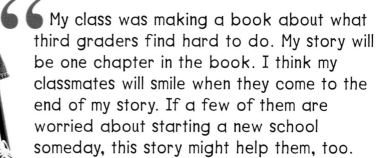

> My class was making a book about what third graders find hard to do. My story will be one chapter in the book. I think my classmates will smile when they come to the end of my story. If a few of them are worried about starting a new school someday, this story might help them, too.
>
> "Since my chapter has dialogue and pictures, the story should come alive for my readers. Here's what I did to publish my story. "

1. First, I checked over my story one more time.
2. Next, I decided where to begin and end each page.
3. I added some pictures.
4. Then I made a chapter cover. I put a title, a picture, and the author's name on it.
5. Finally, I added my chapter to our class book.

The New Boy in School
by Lauren

Tony Leva was worried. The next day would be his first day at Jefferson School.

He and his family had moved in the middle of March. Everyone in the third grade would already know everyone else. Tony was sure that no one would care about a new student. He was also sure that no one would want a new friend. In fact, Tony was so worried that he just sat in his room all day.

The next morning, Tony felt worse. His stomach hurt, and his head hurt, too. He and his mom walked to school. On the way, his mother talked to him. She said, "You'll like your new school, Tony."

Tony didn't feel any better, though. After his mother left, he felt even worse. He walked slowly to his classroom. Lots of students were talking and laughing in the hallway. He didn't know anybody.

Narrative Writing · Realistic Story

Expecting the worst, Tony walked into Ms. Nozawa's classroom. Ms. Nozawa saw him right away and exclaimed, "Wonderful! Here's Tony!" Everyone stopped working. Everyone looked up at Ms. Nozawa and him. Many of the girls and boys smiled. Suddenly, they all started to clap! Ms. Nozawa clapped, too.

Then she said, "Welcome to our class, Tony. Mark will be your partner today. He will answer all your questions. He will be your pal at recess, and then he will eat lunch with you, too."

glue

Tony was so happy he could not speak, but he smiled at everyone. Maybe, thought Tony, he was going to make friends at Jefferson School after all.

USING the Rubric for Assessment

Go to page 86 in the **Practice** the Strategy **Notebook!** Use that rubric to assess Lauren's paper. Try using the rubric to assess your own writing.

NARRATIVE writing

Folktale

In this chapter, you will work with another kind of narrative fiction writing: the **folktale**.

A **folktale** is a story that has been told and retold many times, usually by people from a particular culture. Some folktales have animal characters. The animals act and talk as if they were human.

The story on the next page retells a western African folktale. Read these questions. Then read the folktale. Keep the questions in mind as you read.

 Does the writer get the reader interested in the story by telling the main characters, the setting, and the problem in the first paragraph?

 Does the story have a clear beginning, middle, and end?

 Does the writer use exact words to make the story more interesting?

 Do all of the details and events help tell the story?

 Is the correct form used when an adjective compares two or more things?

Why Spiders Have Thin Waists

retold by Martha Sullivan

Long, long ago, a greedy spider named Anansi lived deep in the jungle in Africa. Anansi could trap his food in his web, but he also liked to eat other animals' food. His waist was fat from all his eating, but he didn't know that would soon change.

One day, Anansi heard that some animals were planning to have special feasts. Mmmm, mmmm, mmmm, he thought. He asked about the feasts, but none of the animals would tell him anything. They didn't want Anansi coming to eat all their food.

Anansi called his children together. He asked them what they knew about the feasts. Anansi's first son told him that Rabbit was holding a feast, but he didn't know when. Anansi quickly made a plan to find out.

He took a thread from his web. He tied one end around his own fat middle and the other end around his son. He told his son to spy on Rabbit. When the feast started, all his son had to do was pull the thread. Then Anansi and his son would go to the feast.

Anansi's daughter told him that the antelopes were having a feast, but she did not know when. Anansi made the same plan with her.

Then Anansi's second son told him that the bullfrogs were having a feast, but he did not know when. Anansi made the same plan with him.

No one could have been more pleased with himself than Anansi! This is the smartest plan ever, he thought.

A few days later, Anansi felt the first tug on his waist. He shouted with joy. Two minutes later, though, he felt another tug. Then he felt a third tug. "Help! Help!" he screamed, but all three threads kept pulling. Anansi was pulled tighter and tighter until he almost fainted. Then suddenly the threads snapped.

After a long while, Anansi felt fine again, but his waist was never the same. All that pulling had made it much smaller. That is why spiders today still have very thin waists.

Using a Rubric

A rubric is a tool that helps you check a piece of writing. It can also help you figure out if your own writing still needs more work.

How do you use a rubric? You assign 1, 2, 3, or 4 points to tell how well you or another writer did certain things.

Remember the questions you read on page 148? Those questions were used to make this rubric.

"Hi! My name is Lu-yin. I'm learning to retell a folktale, too. What did you think of the folktale you just read? Look at this rubric. First, read each question. Next, read the scoring information for each question. Then we'll use the rubric to score the folktale."

Audience

Does the writer get the reader interested in the story by telling the main characters, the setting, and the problem in the first paragraph?

Organization

Does the story have a clear beginning, middle, and end?

Elaboration

Does the writer use exact words to make the story more interesting?

Clarification

Do all of the details and events help tell the story?

Conventions & Skills

Is the correct form used when an adjective compares two or more things?

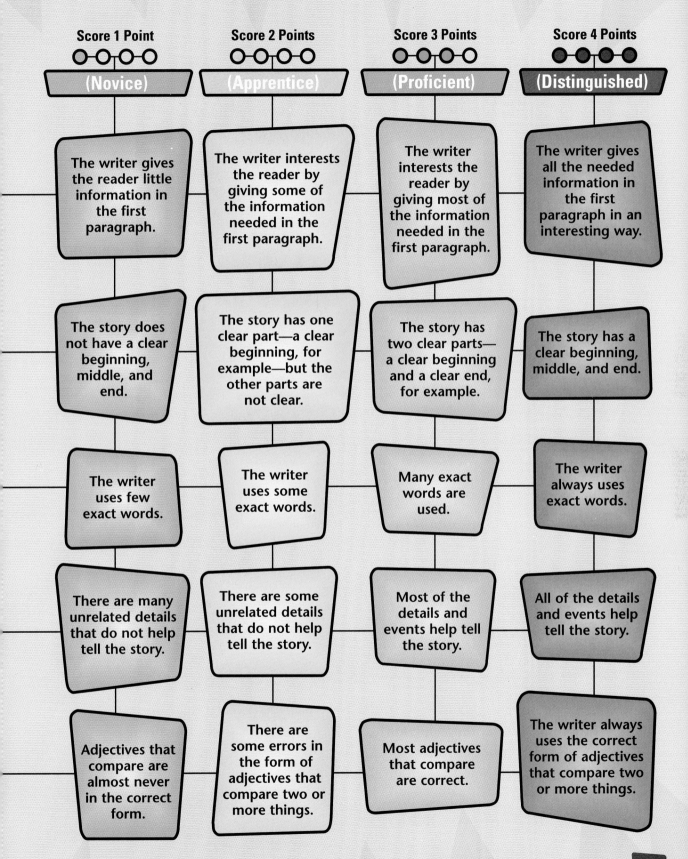

Score 1 Point (Novice)	Score 2 Points (Apprentice)	Score 3 Points (Proficient)	Score 4 Points (Distinguished)
The writer gives the reader little information in the first paragraph.	The writer interests the reader by giving some of the information needed in the first paragraph.	The writer interests the reader by giving most of the information needed in the first paragraph.	The writer gives all the needed information in the first paragraph in an interesting way.
The story does not have a clear beginning, middle, and end.	The story has one clear part—a clear beginning, for example—but the other parts are not clear.	The story has two clear parts—a clear beginning and a clear end, for example.	The story has a clear beginning, middle, and end.
The writer uses few exact words.	The writer uses some exact words.	Many exact words are used.	The writer always uses exact words.
There are many unrelated details that do not help tell the story.	There are some unrelated details that do not help tell the story.	Most of the details and events help tell the story.	All of the details and events help tell the story.
Adjectives that compare are almost never in the correct form.	There are some errors in the form of adjectives that compare two or more things.	Most adjectives that compare are correct.	The writer always uses the correct form of adjectives that compare two or more things.

Using a Rubric to Study the Model

Discuss each question on the rubric with your classmates. Find words and sentences in the folktale that help you answer each one. Use the rubric to give Martha Sullivan's folktale a score for each question.

Audience

Does the writer get the reader interested in the story by telling the main characters, the setting, and the problem in the first paragraph?

"The first paragraph gives important information for the story. It says that the story is about Anansi, the spider, who is the main character. We know right away that the spider is greedy. That's interesting! **Long, long ago** tells when the story takes place. **Africa** tells where it happened. The first paragraph also gives clues as to what the problem is going to be. It hints that something will happen to change the main character's waist. The first paragraph interests the reader in the story!"

Long, long ago, a greedy spider named Anansi lived deep in the jungle in Africa. Anansi could trap his food in his web, but he also liked to eat other animals' food. His waist was fat from all his eating, but he didn't know that would soon change.

Does the story have a clear beginning, middle, and end?

" After the main character, the setting, and the problem are given in the first paragraph, the middle tells about what happens in the story. Here's an example from the middle of the folktale that tells about one event. "

Anansi called his children together. He asked them what they knew about the feasts. Anansi's first son told him that Rabbit was holding a feast, but he didn't know when. Anansi quickly made a plan to find out.

" The last paragraph brings the folktale to a very clear end. "

After a long while, Anansi felt fine again, but his waist was never the same. All that pulling had made it much smaller. That is why spiders today still have very thin waists.

Elaboration

Does the writer use exact words to make the story more interesting?

" Read part of this paragraph. The writer uses the noun **tug**. That's an exact noun. It tells exactly what it was that Anansi felt. The writer also uses the verb **shouted**. The exact verb shows exactly what Anansi was doing and feeling. It tells how loud. It shows emotion. "

A few days later, Anansi felt the first tug on his waist. He shouted with joy. Two minutes later, though, he felt another tug.

Clarification

Do all of the details and events help tell the story?

❝ Read this paragraph. It tells what Anansi did to find out about feasts. Every sentence gives necessary information. The sentences tell everything the reader needs to know. ❞

He took a thread from his web. He tied one end around his own fat middle and the other end around his son. He told his son to spy on Rabbit. When the feast started, all his son had to do was pull the thread. Then Anansi and his son would go to the feast.

Conventions & Skills

Is the correct form used when an adjective compares two or more things?

❝ All the adjectives that compare are in the correct form. For example, in the paragraph below, the writer chooses **more pleased** (not **pleaseder**) and **smartest** (not **most smart**). ❞

No one could have been more pleased with himself than Anansi! This is the smartest plan ever, he thought.

❝ Now it's my turn to write!

I'm going to retell a different folktale. Follow along to see how I practice using good writing strategies and the rubric, too. ❞

Lu-yin

Writer of a Folktale

Name:	Lu-yin
Home:	Rhode Island
Favorite Animal:	monkeys
Favorite Book:	*Gorillas: Gentle Giants of the Forest* by Joyce Milton
Favorite Ways to Spend Time With Friends:	sleepovers, skateboarding, putting on plays and puppet shows
Assignment:	retell a folktale

Prewriting

Gather

Read some folktales. Decide which folktale to retell. Make notes to help me remember the story.

" My class has been reading folktales all month. Folktales are told and heard all over the world. When our teacher asked us to choose one to retell, it wasn't hard for me to decide. I chose the one I had read about a crocodile and a monkey. It is a folktale from India that is more than 2,000 years old. I love monkeys, and the monkey in this story is smart and funny. "

Folktale

Folktales are stories that have been shared and **retold** by people of a particular culture or country. Folktales often tell about a culture's values. When people retell a story, they tell it again, using their own words. Sometimes they make small changes. Most folktales have been told and retold hundreds of times. For that reason, you might hear the same story told in a few different ways.

" I wrote down some things I remember from the story. I may have missed some parts or changed some of it. That's not a problem. Folktales have been told and retold many times. Folktales change a little each time as they are retold. "

First, I wrote down the name of the folktale. Then I wrote down the characters in the story and the problem. From there I just started writing notes about the events. **""**

Folktale: Monkey Tricks Crocodile

Characters: Monkey and Crocodile

Problem: Crocodile is hungry.

Notes:

- Hungry crocodile wants a monkey for dinner.

- Crocodile lives near happy monkeys.

- Monkey can't swim.

- Crocodile plans to drown monkey.

- Crocodile tricks monkey into getting on his back.

- Monkeys live in tree near river.

- Monkey tricks crocodile and escapes.

- Monkey laughs.

- Story takes place long ago and far away.

Go to page 88 in the **Practice** the Strategy **Notebook!**

Prewriting

Organize
Use my notes to make a story map.

> I know from the **Rubric** that my story needs a clear beginning, middle, and end. I'll make a story map to organize the folktale. Then I'll be sure to have those three parts in order.

Story Map

A **story map** organizes the events of a story into a beginning, a middle, and an end. The beginning introduces the characters and the story's problem. The middle tells the main events that happen because of the problem. The end tells how the problem comes out.

> I know the characters in this story are monkeys and crocodiles. The crocodiles are always hungry, and this is a problem. I will put this information in the Beginning box. The crocodile makes a plan and tries to eat the monkey. The monkey has her own plan. These are main events of the story, so I'll put them in the Middle box. The monkey solves her problem of being eaten and escapes. This is how the story comes out in the end. I will put this in the End box.

Beginning

- Long ago, in a faraway place, happy monkeys and unhappy crocodiles lived near each other.

- The monkeys ate well, but the crocodiles were always hungry. (This is the problem.)

Middle

- Crocodile wanted to eat a monkey for dinner. (That would solve the problem for the crocodile, but not the monkey.)

- Crocodile tricked the monkey into getting on his back.

- Crocodile started to swim across the river.

- Crocodile told the monkey that he was going to eat her.

- Monkey tricked Crocodile into taking her back to shore.

End

- Monkey escaped to the tree and laughed at foolish Crocodile. (This is how the problem is solved for the monkey, but not for the crocodile.)

Go to page 91 in the **Practice** the Strategy **Notebook!**

Drafting

Write

Set up the folktale by telling the main characters, setting, and problem in the first paragraph.

> It's time to write my first draft. The **Rubric** reminds me to give important information in my first paragraph. I have to name the main characters and tell where and when the story takes place. Most important, I have to tell my reader what the problem is. That's what the story is really about.
> "I'll also need to follow the story map I made."

Setting

The **setting** is the time and place of a story.

> Here is part of my first draft. I've called my folktale **Smart and Smarter.**

[1st DRAFT]

Smart and Smarter

setting (when and where story takes place)

Long ago, in a faraway place, ~~their~~ there were some **main characters** happy monkeys and some unhappy crocodiles. The monkeys lived in the trees and ate mangoes all day. ~~Crocdiles~~ Crocodiles can live on the land or in the water. The crocodiles lived in the river. They were often hungry. **problem**

One day, a young crocodile decided to catch a monkey and eat it for dinner. He had many crocodile friends who were hungry, ~~two~~ too.

The next day, Crocodile went up to one of the most big, most fat, most happy monkeys. The monkeys reminded him of big birds that fly between trees. He said, "Those mangoes look good, but I know ~~were~~ where you can find more big, more ripe mangoes than those."

Go to page 92 in the **Practice** the Strategy ∧ **Notebook!**

Revising

Elaborate
Add exact words to make the story more interesting.

" The **Rubric** reminds me to use exact words. If I use the right words to retell this folktale, my readers will find it more lively and interesting. That's because exact words give more information.

"I'm going to read what I've written again. I'll ask myself if each word says specifically what I really mean. If it doesn't, I'll try to think of a more exact word. "

[2nd DRAFT]

Exact Words

An **exact** word gives more information than a more general word. For example, the word *woodpecker* is more exact than the more general word *bird*. Following are more examples of general and exact words.

General Words	Exact Words
food	apples
got	grabbed
went	raced
said	called

When Crocodile reached Monkey's home, Monkey said, "My heart is up in that big, tall tree. Just give me a ~~little time,~~ and *exact word* → minute
I'll climb the tree and get it." She ~~got~~ off Crocodile's back *exact word* → leaped
and ran quickly to the top of the tree.

When Monkey reached the highest ~~part~~, she laughed loudly. branch ← *exact word*
"You can't eat me now, Crocodile," she ~~said~~. She thought to called ← *exact word*
herself, what a smart monkey I am!

Go to page 94 in the **Practice** the Strategy **Notebook!**

Revising

Clarify
Take out information that doesn't help tell my story.

" I know from the **Rubric** that I have to take out sentences that don't help tell the story. Zoe read my folktale. She helped me decide what to take out. I'm going to go back to take out the sentences that don't belong. "

Smart and Smarter

[3rd DRAFT]

Long ago, in a faraway place, there were some happy monkeys and some unhappy crocodiles. The monkeys lived in

does not help tell the story →

the trees and ate mangoes all day. Crocodiles can live on the land or in the water. The crocodiles lived in the river. They were often hungry. One day, a young crocodile decided to

does not help tell the story →

catch a monkey and eat it for dinner. He had many crocodile friends who were hungry, too.

The next day, Crocodile went up to one of the most big,

does not help tell the story →

most fat, most happy monkeys. The monkeys reminded him of big birds that fly between trees. He said, "Those mangoes look good, but I know where you can find more big, more ripe mangoes than those."

Go to page 95 in the **Practice** ~the Strategy~ **Notebook!**

Editing

Proofread
Check that the correct form is used when an adjective compares two or more things.

" Now that I've spent time making my folktale clear and lively, I want to check that everything is correct.

"First, I'll proofread my spelling, capitalization, and punctuation. I always do that. The **Rubric** reminds me to use the correct form of adjectives that compare. I'll proofread those adjectives next. "

Adjectives That Compare

To compare two things, add *-er* to most short adjectives.
For most longer adjectives, use the word *more* before the adjective.

To compare more than two things, add *-est* to most short adjectives.
For most longer adjectives, use the word *most* before the adjective.

Comparing Two Things	Comparing Three or More Things
This tree is **taller** than that one.	Here is the **tallest** tree of all.
The clouds are **darker** this afternoon than they were this morning.	That is the **darkest** cloud I've ever seen.
Tricking a monkey is **more difficult** than tricking a crocodile.	Which animal is the **most difficult** to trick?
Mangoes are **more delicious** than apples.	This mango is the **most delicious** fruit I have ever eaten.

Extra Practice
See **Comparing With Adjectives**
(pages CS 16–CS 17) in the back of this book.

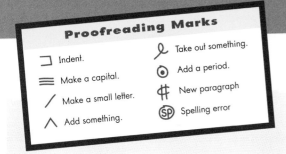

[4th DRAFT]

adjectives that compare three or more things ⟶ biggest,

The next day, Crocodile went up to one of the ~~most big,~~
fattest, happiest
~~most fat, most happy~~ monkeys. He said, "Those mangoes look

good, but I know where you can find ~~more big, more ripe~~
bigger, riper
mangoes than those."

adjectives that
compare two things

Monkey was interested right away. She asked where the
were SP
mangoes ~~wer~~. Crocodile said they were on an island. He told

Monkey that he could easily take her there. All she had to do

was get on Crocodile's back, and he would swim across the river

with her. When Monkey agreed to this plan, Crocodile thought to
himself
~~hisself~~, what a smart crocodile I am!

Crocodile was almost at the island when he told Monkey that

he was going to eat her. Monkey was surprised, but she was not

so surprised that she couldn't think fast. She said in her most

agreeable voice, "Oh, that's too bad. If I had known, I would
most delicious
have brought my heart. That's the ~~deliciousest~~ part of me!"

adjective form that compares three or more things

the Strategy
Go to page 97 in the **Practice**∧**Notebook!**

Publishing

Share
Record my folktale on audiotape for a class radio program.

Writer:	Lu-yin
Assignment:	retell a folktale
Topic:	Monkey tricks Crocodile
Audience:	classmates
Method of Publication:	audiotape
Reason for Choice:	It will be fun to listen to folktales. Besides, folktales used to be told out loud rather than written. We will be following tradition.

" Everyone wanted to hear the folktales that we wrote. Since folktales were first told aloud by storytellers, we decided to put together a radio show so everyone could hear the tales. We each recorded our folktales on an audiotape.

"This is what I did. "

1. First, I checked my folktale one more time to be sure it was exactly the way I wanted.

2. Then I decided how to read my folktale. I decided which parts to read softly or loudly. I decided which parts to read fast or slowly. I thought about whether to sound scared or happy.

3. I practiced reading the folktale aloud with feeling.

4. Afterward, I practiced giving a short introduction to the folktale. I announced the title, the country it came from, and my name.

5. Finally, I worked with my classmates to create a radio show. We all introduced and read our folktales on the tape. It was fun!

Narrative Writing • Folktale

Smart and Smarter
by Lu-yin

Long ago, in a faraway place, there were some happy monkeys and some unhappy crocodiles. The monkeys lived in the trees and ate mangoes all day. The crocodiles lived in the river. They were often hungry. One day, a young crocodile decided to catch a monkey and eat it for dinner.

The next day, Crocodile went up to one of the biggest, fattest, happiest monkeys. He said, "Those mangoes look good, but I know where you can find bigger, riper mangoes than those."

Monkey was interested right away. She asked where the mangoes were. Crocodile said they were on an island. He told Monkey that he could easily take her there. All she had to do was get on

Crocodile's back, and he would swim across the river with her. When Monkey agreed to this plan, Crocodile thought to himself, what a smart crocodile I am!

Crocodile was almost at the island when he told Monkey that he was going to eat her. Monkey was surprised, but she was not so surprised that she couldn't think fast. She said in her most agreeable voice, "Oh, that's too bad. If I had known, I would have brought my heart. That's the most delicious part of me!"

Crocodile didn't want to miss such a tasty part of Monkey. He said in an even more agreeable voice, "That's really no problem, Monkey. I can take you back home. Then you can get your heart for me." So he turned around and swam down the river with Monkey still on his back.

When Crocodile reached Monkey's home, Monkey said, "My heart is up in that big, tall tree. Just give me a minute, and I'll climb the tree and get it." She leaped off Crocodile's back and ran quickly to the top of the tree.

When Monkey reached the highest branch, she laughed loudly. "You can't eat me now, Crocodile," she called. She thought to herself, what a smart monkey I am!

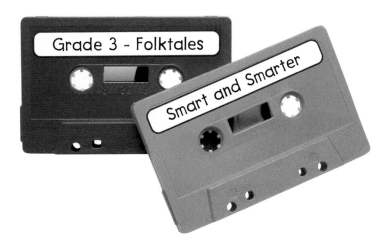

Grade 3 - Folktales

Smart and Smarter

USING the Rubric for Assessment

Go to page 100 in the **Practice the Strategy Notebook!** Use that rubric to assess Lu-yin's paper. Try using the rubric to assess your own writing.

your own NARRATIVE writing
Language Arts

Put the strategies you practiced in this unit to work to write your own realistic story, folktale, or both! You can:

- develop the writing you did in the Your Own Writing pages of the *Practice the Strategy Notebook*;

- pick an idea below and write something new;

- choose another idea of your own.

Be sure to follow the steps in the writing process. Use the rubrics in this unit to assess your writing.

Realistic Story
• the day that you got your first pet • the time someone took a risk that turned out well • a time when someone rescued someone else • a time when you overcame a fear • a time when you helped someone in need

Folktale
• how an animal learns a lesson • why an animal has a feature (for example, why a giraffe has a long neck) • a time when an animal is tricked • how an animal tricks a person • the day a person learns a lesson

portfolio

School–Home Connection

Keep a writing portfolio. Think about adding the activities from the *Practice the Strategy Notebook* to your writing portfolio. You may want to take your portfolio home to share.

PERSUASIVE

writing

states and supports an opinion.

1

Persuasive Paragraph

2

Persuasive Essay

PERSUASIVE writing

Persuasive Paragraph

In this chapter, you will work with one kind of persuasive writing: the **persuasive paragraph**.

A **persuasive paragraph** gives an opinion. The writer wants to persuade others to agree with or act on that opinion.

The paragraph on the next page is a persuasive paragraph. Read these questions. Then read the persuasive paragraph. Keep the questions in mind as you read.

 Does the first sentence let the reader know the writer's opinion?

 Do the middle sentences support the writer's opinion? Does the last sentence restate the opinion?

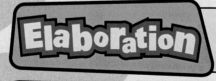 How well does the writer use signal words to make the paragraph easy to understand?

 Has the writer avoided stringy sentences (sentences with too many *and*'s or *so*'s)?

 Are all proper nouns capitalized?

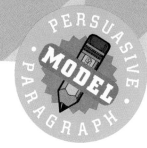
Learning About the Past

by Eva Sanchez

If you are interested in learning about the past, talk to your grandparents or other older people. You will learn about things that are not in history books. For example, you can find out about the everyday problems people faced. They can tell about things they didn't have in their daily lives, like computers and cell phones. They can describe what they ate, how they lived, and what they did for fun. Grandparents can tell us a lot about history, too. Do your grandparents remember the first walk on the moon in 1969? Did they celebrate in 1976? The United States had a big birthday party that year. It turned two hundred! Your grandparents might remember those times. They can tell you what they did and how they felt. Another reason to ask about the past is to get closer to older people. You will feel closer to them because you know more about them. Grandparents or older relatives might tell you about your own family's past. Maybe your family came from another country or state. Older people might be able to describe the place. They might have photos to show you, too. There might be letters to share. You may hear some good stories. If you want to learn about the past, visit some older folks!

Using a Rubric

A rubric is a tool that helps you assess a piece of writing. It can also help you figure out if your own writing still needs more work.

How do you use a rubric? You assign 1, 2, 3, or 4 points to tell how well you or another writer did certain things.

Remember the questions you read on page 174? Those questions were used to make this rubric.

> " Hi! My name is Louis. I'm learning how to write a persuasive paragraph, too. What did you think of the persuasive paragraph you just read? Look at this rubric. First, read each question. Next, read the information for each question. Then we'll use the rubric to assess the persuasive paragraph. "

Audience

Does the first sentence let the reader know the writer's opinion?

Organization

Do the middle sentences support the writer's opinion? Does the last sentence restate the opinion?

Elaboration

How well does the writer use signal words to make the paragraph easy to understand?

Clarification

Has the writer avoided stringy sentences (sentences with too many *and*'s or *so*'s)?

Conventions & Skills

Are all proper nouns capitalized?

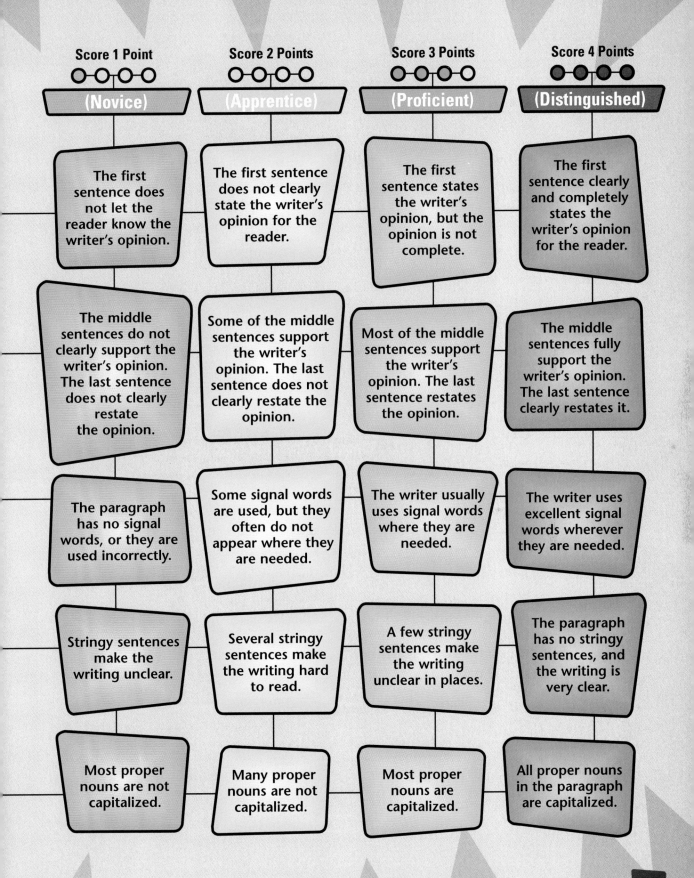

Score 1 Point (Novice)	Score 2 Points (Apprentice)	Score 3 Points (Proficient)	Score 4 Points (Distinguished)
The first sentence does not let the reader know the writer's opinion.	The first sentence does not clearly state the writer's opinion for the reader.	The first sentence states the writer's opinion, but the opinion is not complete.	The first sentence clearly and completely states the writer's opinion for the reader.
The middle sentences do not clearly support the writer's opinion. The last sentence does not clearly restate the opinion.	Some of the middle sentences support the writer's opinion. The last sentence does not clearly restate the opinion.	Most of the middle sentences support the writer's opinion. The last sentence restates the opinion.	The middle sentences fully support the writer's opinion. The last sentence clearly restates it.
The paragraph has no signal words, or they are used incorrectly.	Some signal words are used, but they often do not appear where they are needed.	The writer usually uses signal words where they are needed.	The writer uses excellent signal words wherever they are needed.
Stringy sentences make the writing unclear.	Several stringy sentences make the writing hard to read.	A few stringy sentences make the writing unclear in places.	The paragraph has no stringy sentences, and the writing is very clear.
Most proper nouns are not capitalized.	Many proper nouns are not capitalized.	Most proper nouns are capitalized.	All proper nouns in the paragraph are capitalized.

Using a Rubric to Study the Model

Discuss each question on the rubric with your classmates. Find words and sentences in Eva Sanchez's persuasive paragraph that help you answer each one. Use the rubric to assess the persuasive paragraph on each question.

Audience

Does the first sentence let the reader know the writer's opinion?

"Yes, the first sentence clearly states the writer's opinion. The writer believes we can learn about the past from older people."

If you are interested in learning about the past, talk to your grandparents or other older people.

Do the middle sentences support the writer's opinion? Does the last sentence restate the opinion?

" Yes, the middle sentences give reasons why we should talk about the past to our grandparents and other older people. Those sentences explain the reasons, too. The reasons and explanations **support** the writer's first sentence. Here are some of the middle sentences that support the writer's opinion. "

You will learn about things that are not in history books. For example, you can find out about the everyday problems people faced.

Grandparents can tell us a lot about history, too. . . . Grandparents or older relatives might tell you about your own family's past.

" The last sentence states the writer's opinion again, but it uses different words. "

If you want to learn about the past, visit some older folks!

How well does the writer use signal words to make the paragraph easy to understand?

" Signal words help the reader understand the reasons and explanations that support the writer's opinion. Here the writer uses the signal words **another reason** and **because**. These words help show how ideas are connected. "

Another reason to ask about the past is to get closer to older people. You will feel closer to them because you know more about them.

Clarification

Has the writer avoided stringy sentences (sentences with too many *and*'s or *so*'s)?

"The writer doesn't string sentences together with a lot of **and**'s or **so**'s. Each sentence is clear and easy to understand. Here are some examples.

Grandparents can tell us a lot about history, too. Do your grandparents remember the first walk on the moon in 1969? Did they celebrate in 1976? The United States had a big birthday party that year. It turned two hundred!

Conventions & Skills

Are all proper nouns capitalized?

"Yes, the writer capitalizes proper nouns. In this sentence, she correctly capitalizes the name of our country, the United States."

The United States had a big birthday party that year.

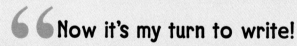

Now it's my turn to write!

I'm going to write my own persuasive paragraph. Follow along to see how I practice using good writing strategies and the rubric, too."

LOUIS

Writer of a Persuasive Paragraph

Name:	Louis
Home:	Texas
Favorite Musical Instrument:	guitar
Favorite Book:	*Baseball Saved Us* by Ken Mochizuki
Hobbies:	music, horseback riding, baseball
Assignment:	persuasive paragraph

Prewriting

Gather

Use interviews to gather information. Take notes and put the answers you get to each question together.

" When my teacher told us to write a persuasive paragraph, I knew right away what I wanted to write about. Every year I go to a celebration called Juneteenth. Juneteenth is the oldest known celebration of the ending of slavery. The very first celebration was held in Texas. Juneteenth got its name from the fact that the slaves were freed in Texas on June 19th. I've heard about other Juneteenth parties, but my opinion is ours is one of the best! "

Opinion

An **opinion** is a belief—often a strong belief—that is based on reasons. Unlike a fact, an opinion cannot be proven to be true.

" I know a lot about our Juneteenth celebration, but I wanted to find out more. I decided to talk to some people in my town, Mexia, Texas. My strategy was to interview them to get more information.

"I interviewed two people, my teacher and my best friend, Bob. Here are my questions and their answers. "

My Interview With My Teacher

1. **Question:** How is our Juneteenth different from other Juneteenth celebrations?

   Answer: Our Juneteenth is special because the first celebration was held right here in Texas in 1898.

2. **Question:** What can you tell me about how the Juneteenth celebration got started in our town?

Answer: Juneteenth celebrates the freedom of the slaves. The freed slaves bought land here in Mexia. They used that piece of land to hold the first Juneteenth celebration. So, today, we use this same piece of land to hold our celebration. It is very historical and special.

3. **Question:** Do you think our town has one of the best Juneteenth celebrations? Why or why not?

   Answer: It is one of the biggest Juneteenth celebrations anywhere in the world.

4. **Question:** What can you do at our Juneteenth celebration?

   Answer: Our Juneteenth celebration is fun and educational, too. We learn new songs and hear stories about the first Juneteenth celebration.

My Interview With Bob

1. **Question:** How is our Juneteenth different from other Juneteenth celebrations?

   Answer: It is better here than anywhere else because it started here.

2. **Question:** What can you tell me about how the Juneteenth celebration got started in our town?

   Answer: We have our celebration on the exact same spot as the freed slaves did.

3. **Question:** Do you think our town has one of the best Juneteenth celebrations? Why or why not?

   Answer: It is one of the biggest celebrations anywhere.

4. **Question:** What can you do at our Juneteenth celebration?

   Anwser: All of my friends come to the celebration. It is fun being together, playing games, and eating.

Prewriting

Gather

Use interviews to gather information. Take notes and put the answers you get to each question together.

"My teacher and Bob gave me some good answers to my interview questions. Now I will write down the main ideas from both interviews after each question. That way I won't forget what I want to write in my paragraph."

My Interview Questions

1. **Question:** How is our Juneteenth different from other Juneteenth celebrations?

   Answer: The first Juneteenth happened here in Texas in 1898. Because it started here, it's very special here.

2. **Question:** What can you tell me about how the Juneteenth celebration got started in our town?

   Answer: The slaves were freed and they used the land they bought here in Mexia, Texas, to celebrate. We use the same land to celebrate today.

3. **Question:** Do you think our town has one of the best Juneteenth celebrations? Why or why not?

   Answer: It is one of the biggest celebrations anywhere.

4. **Question:** What can you do at our Juneteenth celebration?

   Answer: There is a lot to do on Juneteenth in Mexia. It's fun to celebrate this special day with friends. We eat all kinds of interesting food, play games, and learn new songs, too.

Go to page 102 in the Practice the Strategy Notebook!

Prewriting

Organize
Use my notes to make a main-idea table.

" A main-idea table will help me organize my paragraph. My opinion is the main idea of the paragraph. My reasons are the details. They explain or support my opinion.

"In other words, my reasons tell **why** I hold my opinion. The answers I got to my interview questions helped me with some of my reasons. "

Main-Idea Table

A **main-idea table** shows how a main idea is supported by details. The details "hold up" or support the main idea.

Main Idea (My Opinion):

The best Juneteenth Celebration is in Mexia, Texas.

Supporting Detail (a reason)	Supporting Detail (a reason)	Supporting Detail (a reason)	Supporting Detail (a reason)
Juneteenth began in Texas, so it's special here.	Mexia, Texas, has celebrated Juneteeth since 1898, so it means a lot to the town.	The party is one of the biggest anywhere!	There are many exciting things to do.

Go to page 104 in the **Practice** the Strategy **Notebook!**

Drafting

Write

State my opinion in the first sentence. Support my opinion in the middle of the paragraph. Restate my opinion in the last sentence.

" Now I can start writing. I need to convince my audience that my opinion makes sense.

"From the **Rubric** I know that the first sentence should state my opinion for the reader. That's the same as my main idea, and I can take that sentence straight from my main-idea table.

"The middle of my paragraph has to support my opinion. I can take the supporting details (my reasons) from my main-idea table. Then I'll explain each reason in my draft.

"I'll end my paragraph with a sentence that restates my main idea (my opinion). This time I'll say it in different words. "

Louis's
opinion

Juneteenth in Mexia

reasons

One of the best places to go for Juneteenth is Mexia, Texas.
Juneteenth started in texas. Juneteenth is named for june 19,
1865, and slavery ended in Texas on that day, and the day is
special in Texas, and it is extra special in mexia. The holiday ~~is~~
has been held here for such a long time. Slaves who were
freed in Mexia joined together, and they ~~decided~~ bought land,
and they used the land to celebrate juneteenth, and that took
place in 1898. Today people ~~are~~ still use the same land for
Juneteenth. Mexia's Juneteenth is awesome also one of the
best because it is so big. It might be the bigest celebration
anywhere. One year, 20,000 people came. They ate, slept,
sang, and had a big party. Juneteenth is a lot of fun.
Juneteenth in Mexia, Texas is one of the biggest and best
celebrations in the world. ◄── **Louis's restated opinion**

Go to page 106 in the **Practice** **Notebook!**
the Strategy

Revising

Elaborate
Add signal words that make my paragraph easy to understand.

" The **Rubric** reminds me to add signal words. Signal words will help the reader understand my paragraph better. Those words will connect the sentences that don't seem tied to other sentences. "

Signal Words

A **signal word** helps tie ideas together. It guides the reader from one idea to another. Here are some words and groups of words that are used as signals in persuasive writing.

- as a result
- because
- for this reason
- in fact
- one reason is that
- that is because
- the reason why
- therefore

[2nd DRAFT]

signal words

One of the best places to go for Juneteenth is Mexia, Texas. One reason is that Juneteenth started in texas. Juneteenth is named for june 19, 1865, and slavery ended in Texas on that day, and the day is special in Texas, and it is extra special in signal words mexia. That is because The holiday has been held here for signal words such a long time. In fact, Slaves who were freed in Mexia joined together, and they bought land, and they used the land to celebrate juneteenth, and that took place in 1898.

Go to page 109 in the **Practice** the Strategy **Notebook!**

ReVising

Clarify
Look for stringy sentences and separate them.

66 I read my first and second drafts. Then I looked back at the questions on the **Rubric**. One of them reminded me to look for stringy sentences. I found some. I will break them up into shorter sentences that are clearer to read and easier to understand. 99

READ TO
MYSELF

Stringy Sentences

Stringy sentences use too many *and*'s or *so*'s. A stringy sentence is so long that it has too many different parts or ideas in it. Stringy sentences should be separated into shorter sentences.

Stringy: The celebration includes balloon rides, and there are games, and children play horseshoes, and everyone has fun.

Better: The celebration includes balloon rides and games. Children play horseshoes, and everyone has fun.

---

shorter sentences from a stringy sentence

[3rd DRAFT]

Juneteenth is named for june 19, 1865, and slavery ended in

Texas on that day, and the day is special in Texas, and it is

extra special in mexia. That is because The holiday has been
shorter sentences from a stringy sentence
held here for such a long time. In fact, Slaves who were freed

in Mexia joined together, and they bought land, and they used

the land to celebrate juneteenth, and that took place in 1898.

Go to page 110 in the **Practice** the Strategy **Notebook!**

Editing

Proofread   Check that all proper nouns have been capitalized.

" Now I need to check for errors. First, I'll check spelling, capitalization, and punctuation. I always do that. Then I'll reread my paragraph to make sure I capitalized all proper nouns. "

Proper Nouns

A **proper noun** is the name of a specific person, place, or thing. Proper nouns are always capitalized.

- Capitalize a specific person: **G**randma **E**dna, **G**randpa **C**larence
- Capitalize a specific place: **A**nn **A**rbor, **M**ichigan
- Capitalize specific days of the week: **F**riday
- Capitalize specific months of the year: **A**pril
- Capitalize specific things: **T**eton **M**ountains

Extra Practice
See **Proper Nouns**
(pages CS 18–CS 19) in the back of this book.

[4th DRAFT]

Juneteenth in Mexia

One of the best places to go for Juneteenth is Mexia, Texas.
One reason is that Juneteenth started in texas. ← **proper noun** Juneteenth is
named for june 19, 1865. ← **proper noun** Slavery ended in Texas on that day. The
day is special in Texas, and it is extra special in mexia. ← **proper noun** That is
because The holiday has been held here for such a long time. In
fact, Slaves who were freed in Mexia joined together. They
bought land, and they used the land to celebrate juneteenth. ← **proper noun**
That took place in 1898. Today people still use the same land for
Juneteenth. Mexia's Juneteenth is also one of the best because it
is so big. It might be the bigest g SP celebration anywhere. One year,
∧
20,000 people came. They ate, slept, sang, and had a big party.
Juneteenth is a lot of fun. Juneteenth in Mexia, Texas, is one of
the biggest and best celebrations in the world.

Go to page 111 in the **Practice** the Strategy ∧ **Notebook!**

Publishing

Share

Post my paragraph on a Class Opinions bulletin board.

Writer:	Louis
Assignment:	persuasive paragraph
Topic:	Juneteenth in Mexia, Texas
Audience:	classmates
Method of Publication:	Class Opinions bulletin board
Reason for Choice:	Everyone in the class can read my opinion.

66 Everyone in my class wrote about something different. We thought it would be fun to read opinions on many topics. That's why we made a bulletin board and called it **Class Opinions**. Here's what I did to publish my persuasive paragraph. 99

1. I checked my persuasive paragraph one more time.
2. I made a border for my paper. I did this by adding strips of colored paper to the edges.
3. When I was finished, I tacked my paper to the bulletin board.

Juneteenth in Mexia

by Louis

One of the best places to go for Juneteenth is Mexia, Texas. One reason is that Juneteenth started in Texas. Juneteenth is named for June 19, 1865. Slavery ended in Texas on that day. The day is special in Texas, and it is extra special in Mexia. That is because the holiday has been held here for such a long time. In fact, slaves who were freed in Mexia joined together. They bought land, and they used the land to celebrate Juneteenth. That took place in 1898. Today people still use the same land for Juneteenth. Mexia's Juneteenth is also one of the best because it is so big. It might be the biggest celebration anywhere. One year, 20,000 people came. They ate, slept, sang, and had a big party. Juneteenth is a lot of fun. Juneteenth in Mexia, Texas, is one of the biggest and best celebrations in the world.

USING the Rubric for Assessment

Go to page 112 in the **Practice** the Strategy **Notebook!** Use that rubric to assess Louis's paper. Try using the rubric to assess your own writing.

PERSUASIVE writing

Persuasive Essay

In this chapter, you will work with another kind of persuasive writing: the **persuasive essay**.

Like a persuasive paragraph, a **persuasive essay** states an opinion. In the essay, the writer tries to persuade the reader to agree with or act on that opinion. A persuasive essay has several paragraphs.

The essay on the next page is a persuasive essay. Read these questions. Then read the persuasive essay. Keep the questions in mind as you read.

 Does the introduction state the writer's opinion clearly to the reader?

 Is there a paragraph for each reason? Does the conclusion restate the opinion?

 Does the writer use enough facts to back up each reason?

 Does the writer include only facts and details that support the opinion?

 Do the subject and verb in each sentence agree?

A Great Career

by Emily Joad

People should think hard when they decide on a career. They should choose a job they will like. They should choose a job that is important and needed. For people who like to help others, nursing is a great career.

One reason to choose nursing is that it is very important work. When someone is sick, a nurse often takes care of the person. A nurse is with a patient much more often than a doctor is. Without nurses to take care of patients, doctors would not be able to do their jobs. Because they watch over patients, nurses can get a person emergency help if it is needed. Nurses often affect how fast people get well. A nurse's good care and kind attitude can help a patient heal. In some cases, nurses save lives.

A second reason to choose nursing is that nurses are needed in many different places. It is easy to find work. Nurses work in hospitals and in doctors' offices. They work at health agencies and in schools. Some nursing jobs are in the military. Others are in industry. Many jobs are in home health care. Sometimes a nurse chooses to teach nursing. Some nurses give advice on how to live a healthy life.

Nursing is a job that matters. We can imagine the world without some jobs, but we cannot imagine the world without nurses. Almost everyone needs a nurse at some time in life. A career in nursing can make a person proud.

Using a Rubric

A rubric is a tool that helps you check a piece of writing. It can also help you figure out if your own writing still needs more work.

How do you use a rubric? You assign 1, 2, 3, or 4 points to tell how well you or another writer did certain things.

Remember the questions you read on page 194? Those questions were used to make this rubric.

"Hi! My name is Luke. I'm learning how to write a persuasive essay, too. What did you think of the essay you just read? Look at this rubric. First, read each question. Next, read the scoring information for each question. Then we'll use the rubric to check the persuasive essay."

Audience
Does the introduction state the writer's opinion clearly to the reader?

Organization
Is there a paragraph for each reason? Does the conclusion restate the opinion?

Elaboration
Does the writer use enough facts to back up each reason?

Clarification
Does the writer include only facts and details that support the opinion?

Conventions & Skills
Do the subject and verb in each sentence agree?

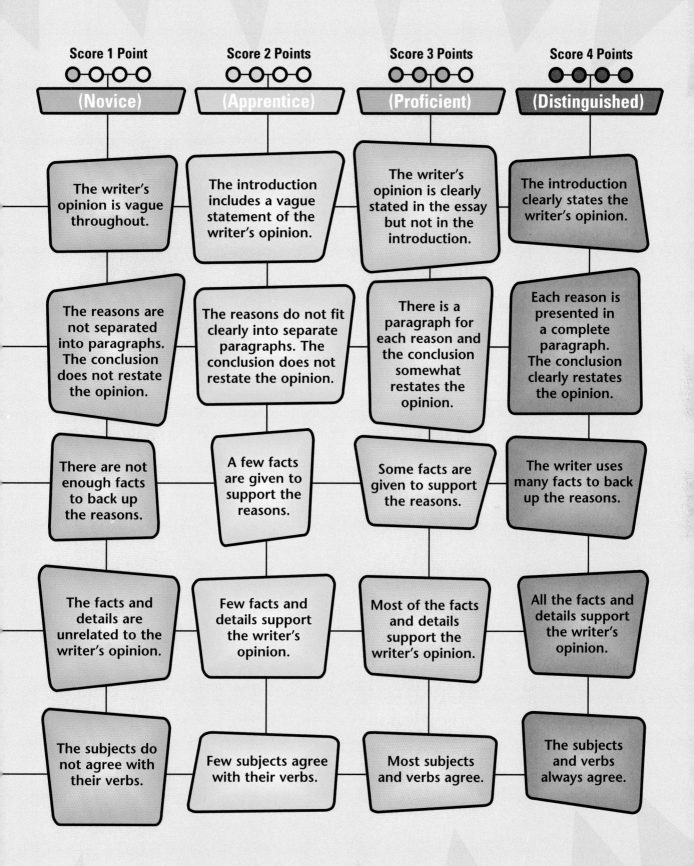

Score 1 Point
(Novice)

The writer's opinion is vague throughout.

The reasons are not separated into paragraphs. The conclusion does not restate the opinion.

There are not enough facts to back up the reasons.

The facts and details are unrelated to the writer's opinion.

The subjects do not agree with their verbs.

Score 2 Points
(Apprentice)

The introduction includes a vague statement of the writer's opinion.

The reasons do not fit clearly into separate paragraphs. The conclusion does not restate the opinion.

A few facts are given to support the reasons.

Few facts and details support the writer's opinion.

Few subjects agree with their verbs.

Score 3 Points
(Proficient)

The writer's opinion is clearly stated in the essay but not in the introduction.

There is a paragraph for each reason and the conclusion somewhat restates the opinion.

Some facts are given to support the reasons.

Most of the facts and details support the writer's opinion.

Most subjects and verbs agree.

Score 4 Points
(Distinguished)

The introduction clearly states the writer's opinion.

Each reason is presented in a complete paragraph. The conclusion clearly restates the opinion.

The writer uses many facts to back up the reasons.

All the facts and details support the writer's opinion.

The subjects and verbs always agree.

Using a Rubric to Study the Model

Discuss each question on the rubric with your classmates. Find words and sentences in the persuasive essay that help you answer each one. Use the rubric to give Emily Joad's persuasive essay a score for each question.

Audience

Does the introduction state the writer's opinion clearly to the reader?

" Yes. The introduction clearly states the writer's opinion. Her opinion is that nursing is a great career for people who like to help others. "

> People should think hard when they decide on a career. They should choose a job they will like. They should choose a job that is important and needed. For people who like to help others, nursing is a great career.

**Is there a paragraph for each reason?
Does the conclusion restate the opinion?**

66 Yes, there is a paragraph for each reason. Everything in this paragraph, for example, tells why nursing is such important work. 99

One reason to choose nursing is that it is very important work. When someone is sick, a nurse often takes care of the person. A nurse is with a patient much more often than a doctor is. Without nurses to take care of patients, doctors would not be able to do their jobs. Because they watch over patients, nurses can get a person emergency help if it is needed. Nurses often affect how fast people get well. A nurse's good care and kind attitude can help a patient heal. In some cases, nurses save lives.

66 The conclusion restates the writer's opinion using different words. 99

Nursing is a job that matters.

Elaboration

Does the writer use enough facts to back up each reason?

66 Yes, the writer uses enough facts to back up each reason. In this example, the writer gives facts about the many different places nurses can work. These facts support the reason why nurses are needed, and why it would be easy for new nurses to find work. 99

It is easy to find work. Nurses work in hospitals and in doctors' offices. They work at health agencies and in schools. Some nursing jobs are in the military. Others are in industry.

Clarification

Does the writer include only facts and details that support the opinion?

" The writer has only included facts and details that support the writer's opinion. Here the writer continues to give specific examples of the many places a nurse can work. "

Many jobs are in home health care. Sometimes a nurse chooses to teach nursing. Some nurses give advice on how to live a healthy life.

Conventions & Skills

Do the subject and verb in each sentence agree?

" Yes, the subject and verb in every sentence agree. Here the writer uses the verb **is** to agree with the singular subject **It**. "

It is easy to find work.

" Now it's my turn to write!

I'm going to write my own persuasive essay. Follow along to see how I use the rubric and practice good writing strategies, too. "

LUKE

Writer of a Persuasive Essay

Name: Luke
Home: Utah
Favorite Sport: cross-country running
Favorite Book: *Come Back Salmon: How a Group of Dedicated Kids Adopted Pigeon Creek and Brought It Back to Life* by Molly Cone
Favorite Things to Do With Friends: touch football, computer games
Assignment: persuasive essay

Prewriting

Gather

Choose a topic about which I have a strong opinion. Make notes on the reasons for my opinion.

" My mom and I run every morning before school. I love running. I think it's the best exercise anyone can do. And, like my mom says, it doesn't cost very much!

"When my teacher asked us to think about something important to us, I thought about running. I made notes on the reasons why I believe that running is the best sport for students. "

Reasons

Reasons tell why. They explain the writer's opinion. In persuasive writing, good reasons help the reader agree with the writer's opinion.

My Opinion: Running is the best sport for students.

My Reasons:

- no gym fees
- can be done almost anytime (morning, afternoon, evening)
- makes you feel great
- keeps you in good shape
- no traveling
- need only running shoes
- no equipment
- can be done almost anywhere (don't need a gym, field, court, pool)
- not that expensive

Go to page 114 in the **Practice** the Strategy **Notebook!**

Persuasive Writing • Persuasive Essay

Prewriting

Organize
Use my notes to make a network tree.

" I know from the **Rubric** that I need good reasons to back up my opinion. My reasons should be facts that support my opinion. I reread my list of reasons. I noticed that my reasons fall into two big categories: You can run almost anywhere, anytime; and it isn't expensive. The rest of my reasons are smaller facts that fit into these categories. I think I will use a network tree to help me organize my notes into these categories. I can organize the two big reasons and then all of the smaller facts that fall under each reason. "

Network Tree

A **network tree** organizes information. For a persuasive essay, the opinion goes at the top of the tree. Reasons for the opinion go on the next level. Facts and other details go on the lowest level.

My Opinion
Running is the best sport for students.

Reason 1
You can run almost anywhere, anytime.

Reason 2
It isn't expensive.

Fact
You don't have to belong to a gym.

Fact
You can run morning, afternoon, or evening.

Fact
You need only running shoes.

Fact
You don't need special clothes or equipment.

Fact
You don't need a field, court, or pool.

Fact
No travel is needed.

Go to page 116 in the **Practice** the Strategy **Notebook!**

Drafting

Write

Draft my essay. Write one paragraph for the introduction. Write one paragraph for the first reason and one paragraph for the second reason. Write one paragraph for the conclusion.

" Now I can start writing. I know from the **Rubric** that I'll need at least four paragraphs—an introduction, at least two middle paragraphs, and a conclusion.

"The first paragraph is the introduction. It should include my opinion, so I'll start with that. The next two paragraphs will explain my two reasons. I'll use my network tree to help me with those paragraphs. Then I'll write a conclusion. I'll put my opinion in the conclusion, too, but I'll use different words. You can read part of my first draft on the next page. "

Introduction

An **introduction** is the first paragraph of a paper. In persuasive writing, the introduction includes the writer's opinion.

My Opinion: Running is the best sport for students.

My Reasons:

Paragraph 1: It can be done almost anywhere and at any time.

Paragraph 2: It is not expensive.

My Restated Opinion: A student just can't find a better sport than running.

Conclusion

A **conclusion** restates the writer's opinion using different words.

Persuasive Writing • Persuasive Essay

The Best Exercise

[1st DRAFT]

introduction

Exercise is important. Adults needs exercise, and ~~you~~ yunger people do, too. Young people can't always do the same exercise that adults do, though. They need something easy and cheap. Running is the best sport for students.

— Luke's opinion

body

Reason 1

Running is a great sport for students because it can be done almost anywhere and at any time. I have been a runner for almost a year now! Runners don't have to ~~go~~ belong to a gym. Students who run don't need a soccer field, a basketball court, or a pool. All they need is a safe place.

On weekends, they can go in the middle of the day. Students ~~can't~~ shouldn't run down the hallway, though.

Reason 2

Another reason why running is the best sport for students is that it is not expensive. The only important item are a pair of good running shoes. Once a person has these, there are no other costs. Runners don't need any special clothes either. No one worries about running ~~every~~ too often or too many times because it costs too much. Runners runs for free.

conclusion

Running, like many sports, has many benefits. It help people stay in shape. It feel good all over. Unlike many other sports, though, running doesn't need a special time or place. Once you have the shoes, it cost nothing. A student just can't find a better sport than running. **Luke's opinion stated in other words**

Go to page 118 in the **Practice** the Strategy **Notebook!**

Revising

Elaborate — Add facts to back up my reasons.

" The **Rubric** reminds me that I need enough facts to back up my reasons. When I checked my essay, I noticed that my first reason was backed up by more facts than my second reason. I decided to add more facts to support my second reason. "

[2nd DRAFT]

Another reason why running is the best sport for students is that it is not expensive. The only important item are a pair of good running shoes. Once a person has these, there are no

facts to support the reason →

other costs. Runners do not have to buy tickets the way skiers do. They don't have to own high-cost items like bicycles or golf clubs. They also don't have to pay to go to some faraway place. Runners don't need any special clothes either.

← **fact to support the reason**

Most people do just fine in a shirt and a pair of shorts. No one worries about running too often or too many times because it costs too much. Runners runs for free.

Go to page 120 in the **Practice** the Strategy **Notebook!**

Revising

Clarify
Take out facts and details that do not support my opinion.

> When Todd read my persuasive essay, he thought about the **Rubric**. He said two of my sentences didn't back up my opinion.
>
> "I decided that Todd was right. I'll go back and cross out those two sentences. "

READ TO A PARTNER

[3rd DRAFT]

Running is a great sport for students because it can be done

does not support the opinion ⟶ almost anywhere and at any time. I have been a runner for almost

a year now! Runners don't have to belong to a gym. Students

who run don't need a soccer field, a basketball court, or a pool.

All they need is a safe place. That place might be right outside

their door. It might be just down the street. Also, running is a

sport that can be done at any time of day. For example, most

swimmers can swim only when a pool is open, but runners can run

at any time. On weekdays, students can run early in the morning.

They can also run after school. On weekends, they can go in the

middle of the day. Students shouldn't run down the hallway,

though. **does not support the opinion**

Go to page 121 in the **Practice** the Strategy **Notebook!**

Editing

Proofread
Check that subjects and verbs always agree.

> I always check my writing for mistakes in spelling, capitalization, and punctuation. The **Rubric** reminds me that I should look at subject-verb agreement, too.
>
> "I'll check each sentence to be sure that every subject and verb agree."
>
> "Look on the next page to see how I corrected this part of my essay."

Conventions & SKILLS

Subject-Verb Agreement

In the present tense, subjects must agree with verbs in number (singular or plural). Singular nouns and some singular pronouns take verbs that end in *-s* or *-es*.

> S   V   S   V   S   V
> **John skis.** The **cat watches**. **She wants** dinner.

Plural nouns and plural pronouns take verbs that do not end in *-s* or *-es*.

> S   V   S   V   S   V
> **They ski.** The **cats watch**. **We want** dinner.

Use *is* or *was* after a singular subject.

> S V   S   V
> **Ann is** a runner. **She was** the winner of the race.

Use *are* or *were* after a plural subject.

> S   V   S   V
> The **boys are** swimmers. **They were** on a swim team.

Extra Practice
See **Subject-Verb Agreement** (pages CS 20–CS 21) in the back of this book.

Proofreading Marks

⌐ Indent.
≡ Make a capital.
/ Make a small letter.
∧ Add something.
ℓ Take out something.
⊙ Add a period.
New paragraph
SP Spelling error

[4th DRAFT]

The Best Exercise

subject-verb agreement ———→ s   younger SP

Exercise is important. Adults needs exercise, and yunger

people do, too. Young people can't always do the same

exercise that adults do, though. They need something easy

and cheap. Running is the best sport for students.

Another reason why running is the best sport for students is

subject-verb agreement ———→ is

that it is not expensive. The only important item are a pair of

good running shoes. Once a person has these, there are no

other costs.

No one worries about running too often or too many times

subject-verb agreement ———→   subject-verb
because it costs too much. Runners runs for free.   agreement
                                                      s
Running, like many sports, has many benefits. It help people

subject-verb agreement ——→ s

stay in shape. It feel good all over. Unlike many other sports,

though, running doesn't need a special time or place. Once you

s ←— subject-verb agreement

have the shoes, it cost nothing. A student just can't find a

better sport than running.

Go to page 122 in the **Practice** the Strategy **Notebook!**

Publishing

Share
Publish my persuasive essay on the class Web site.

Writer: Luke
Assignment: persuasive essay
Topic: why running is the best sport for students
Audience: everyone in the school
Method of Publication: class Web site
Reason for Choice: Everyone can find and read my essay on the Web site.

" Each student in my class wrote about a different topic. We wanted everyone in the school to be able to read our essays. That's why we put them on our class Web site. Here's what I did to publish my persuasive essay. "

1. First, I checked my essay one more time to be sure it had no errors.

2. Then I loaded my document on the class Web site.

3. Finally, I added the title of my paper and my name to the list of persuasive essays on the Web site.

The Best Exercise
by Luke

Exercise is important. Adults need exercise, and younger people do, too. Young people can't always do the same exercise that adults do, though. They need something easy and cheap. Running is the best sport for students.

Running is a great sport for students because it can be done almost anywhere and at any time. Runners don't have to belong to a gym. Students who run don't need a soccer field, a basketball court, or a pool. All they need is a safe place. That place might be right outside their door. It might be just down the street. Also, running is a sport that can be done at any time of day. For example, most swimmers can swim only when a pool is open, but runners can run at any time. On weekdays, students can run early in the morning. They can also run after school. On weekends, they can go in the middle of the day.

Another reason why running is the best sport for students is that it is not expensive. The only important item is a pair of good running shoes. Once a person has these, there are no other costs. Runners do not have to buy tickets the way skiers do. They don't have to own high-cost items like bicycles or golf clubs. They also don't have to pay to go to some faraway place. Runners don't need any special clothes either. Most people do just fine in a shirt and a pair of shorts. No one worries about running too often or too many times because it costs too much. Runners run for free.

Running, like many sports, has many benefits. It helps people stay in shape. It feels good all over. Unlike many other sports, though, running doesn't need a special time or place. Once you have the shoes, it costs nothing. A student just can't find a better sport than running.

USING the Rubric for Assessment

Go to page 124 in the **Practice Notebook!** the Strategy Use that rubric to assess Luke's paper. Try using the rubric to assess your own writing.

your own PERSUASIVE writing

Math

Put the strategies you practiced in this unit to work to write your own persuasive paragraph, persuasive essay, or both! You can:

- develop the writing you did in the Your Own Writing pages of the *Practice the Strategy Notebook*;

- pick an idea below and write something new;

- choose another idea of your own.

Be sure to follow the steps in the writing process. Use the rubrics in this unit to assess your paper.

Persuasive Paragraph	Persuasive Essay
• the best bargain or value in a store • shorter or longer school days • best class fundraiser (profits) • better shape and size of school playground • which exercises burn the most calories	• why a job that uses math (banker, builder, chef) is a great job • why some foods are more healthful than others (nutritional information—use numbers) • why one season is the best season of the year (temperature, amount of rain, number of sunny days)

portfolio

School–Home Connection

Keep a writing portfolio. Think about adding the activities from the *Practice the Strategy Notebook* to your writing portfolio. You may want to take your portfolio home to share.

TEST
writing

measures how well you can present your ideas on a certain topic.

Test Writing

- ☑ starts with a writing prompt.
- ☑ may not let writers use outside sources.
- ☑ may have a time limit.
- ☑ may not allow writers to recopy.

TEST writing

Study the Writing Prompt

Every writing test starts with a writing prompt. Even though they aren't labeled, most writing prompts have three parts: the Setup, the Task, and the Scoring Guide. Read the writing prompt below carefully. Can you find the Setup, the Task, and the Scoring Guide?

Have you ever done something nice for another person? Has someone else done something nice for you? Think about one of these times.

Write a story. You can choose whether to write a story about something nice you did for somebody else or a story about when somebody did something nice for you. Be sure your writing

- gets the audience's attention at the beginning and keeps it throughout the story.
- tells the events in the order they happen.
- includes details to help your reader picture the characters and events.
- clearly tells who or what the story is about and when and where it takes place.
- uses the conventions of language and spelling correctly.

Most writing prompts have three parts:

This part of the writing prompt gives you the background information you need to get ready for writing.

Have you ever done something nice for another person? Has someone else done something nice for you? Think about one of these times.

This part of the writing prompt tells you exactly what you're supposed to write: a story about what happened.

Write a story. You can choose whether to write a story about something nice you did for somebody else or a story about when somebody did something nice for you.

This section tells how your writing will be scored. To do well on the test, you should include everything on the list.

Be sure your writing
• gets the audience's attention at the beginning and keeps it throughout the story.
• tells the events in the order they happen.
• includes details to help your reader picture the characters and events.
• clearly tells who or what the story is about and when and where it takes place.
• uses the conventions of language and spelling correctly.

Using the
Scoring Guide
to Study the Model

❝ Hi. I'm Lucy. Like you, I sometimes have to take a writing test. I pay close attention to the Scoring Guide in the writing prompt.

"Remember the rubrics you've been using in this book? Each one told you what a piece of writing needs to be considered **Novice, Apprentice, Proficient,** or **Distinguished**. ❞

❝ When you take a writing test, you don't always have all that information handy. You just have the basics. But the rubrics you've been using in this book have helped you learn how to pay attention to the most important areas in your writing: **Audience, Organization, Elaboration, Clarification,** and **Conventions & Skills**.

"On the next page, you can see what one student wrote in response to the writing prompt on page 214. You can tell that the student tried to keep the Scoring Guide in mind as she wrote! After you read this story, we'll use the Scoring Guide in the writing prompt to check how well she did. ❞

My New Best Friend

by Tara Kim

It always pays to be nice to people. Sometimes being nice can even bring you a best friend. Let me tell you about a time that someone was really nice to me.

When I was in first grade, I moved to a new school. On my first day, I didn't know a single person, either in my class or in my new neighborhood.

My teacher, Ms. Grasso, told me I would like our class. Still, I felt scared. I didn't know where to go for lunch or where the gym was. I couldn't find the library or the nurse's office on my own. I wasn't sure where to get off the school bus at the end of the day. I was so worried, I thought I might cry in front of the other kids in my class.

On the second day, something really good happened. In Ms. Grasso's class, you get to use a special set of colored pencils on your birthday. Also, you get to pick a friend to share them with you. It was Chandra's birthday and her turn to use the special pencils. She picked me to be the person to share the pencils with her. I was really surprised, because I didn't even know her name then!

While we were drawing, we found out we liked a lot of the same things. We both like to look at stars out our windows. Another thing we both like is riding bikes and making forts. Believe it or not, we both have a hamster named Nibble and a fish named Goldie! Isn't that funny? Once we found out all the things we both like to do, we started playing together almost every day after school.

Chandra is always nice to other people. I learned a good lesson from her. It pays to be nice to everyone. That's how we all will find our new best friends.

66 Look at each point on the Scoring Guide. Then look at the story Tara wrote. See if you can find examples to show how well she did on each part of the Scoring Guide. 99

The writer gets the audience's attention at the beginning and keeps it throughout the story.

Audience

66 This part of the **Scoring Guide** is about the audience. Tara starts out by saying that it pays to be nice. That got my attention. I wondered why she said that, so I wanted to keep on reading. 99

It always pays to be nice to people. Sometimes being nice can even bring you a best friend. Let me tell you about a time that someone was really nice to me.

66 Everything Tara wrote was about someone being nice. She kept my attention by telling all about what happened. 99

> This part of the **Scoring Guide** is about how she organized her writing. It looks like Tara started at the beginning and went from the first thing that happened to the next. Don't you think she did a good job telling about the events in order?

When I was in first grade, I moved to a new school. On my first day, I didn't know a single person, either in my class or in my new neighborhood.

On the second day, something really good happened.

> I see how she used words like **When I was in first grade, On my first day,** and **On the second day** to help show the order of events.

The writer includes details to help the reader picture the characters and events.

Elaboration

> Adding details helps make everything clearer and more interesting. Can you find the details Tara included in this part of her story?

We both like to look at stars out our windows. Another thing we both like is riding bikes and making forts. Believe it or not, we both have a hamster named Nibble and a fish named Goldie!

On the second day, something really good happened. . . . It was Chandra's birthday and her turn to use the special pencils. She picked me to be the person to share the pencils with her. I was really surprised, because I didn't even know her name then!

Once we found out all the things we both like to do, we started playing together almost every day after school.

" Now I'm ready to write!

Let me show you some strategies that will make things easier the next time you take a writing test. Let's take a look at another writing prompt and see how well I do! "

Lucy

Test Writing Champ

Name:	Lucy
Favorite Subject:	social studies
Favorite Book:	*Storm in the Night* by Mary Stolz
Hobbies:	knitting, playing soccer
Assignment:	writing a narrative essay for a test

Prewriting

Gather

Read the writing prompt. Make sure I understand what I am supposed to do.

" Let's look together at a piece of writing I am doing for a test. That will help you work on your own writing test strategies. Of course, the first thing writers do when they write is gather some ideas. When you write to take a test, you start gathering ideas from the writing prompt. Ideas for writing can come from your own knowledge and experiences.

"It's really important to study the writing prompt carefully. You've got to be able to read the prompt without the labels and know exactly what you're supposed to do.

"Here's the writing prompt I have: "

Setup
Suppose you got or gave someone a special gift. What if something surprising happened because of the gift?

Task
Write a story about what happened because of the special gift. Your story may be about something real or make-believe. Be sure your story

Scoring Guide
- gets the audience's attention at the beginning and keeps it throughout the story.
- tells the events in the order they happen.
- includes details to help your reader picture the characters and events.
- clearly tells who or what the story is about and when and where it takes place.
- uses the conventions of language and spelling correctly.

> Before I do anything else, I take five minutes to really study the writing prompt. I follow these steps so I know what to do:

1 Read all three parts of the prompt carefully.

> All right, I found the **Setup**, the **Task**, and the **Scoring Guide**.

2 Circle key words in the Task part of the prompt that tell what kind of writing I need to do and who my audience is.

> I circled the words **Write a story**. That's the kind of writing I will do. I also circled the words **about what happened** to remind me of what I must include. It doesn't say who the audience is, so I'll write for my teacher.

3 Make sure I know how I'll be graded.

> The **Scoring Guide** part tells what I need to include to get a good score. I need to remember that!

4 Say what I need to do in my own words.

> Here's what I need to do. I need to write a story about what happened when I got or gave a special gift.

Go to page 126 in the **Practice** the Strategy **Notebook!**

Prewriting

Organize
Plan my time.

"Prewriting is a little different when you take a test. You need to keep an eye on the clock! Think about how much time you have in all. Then divide the time into the different parts of the writing process. If the test takes an hour, here's how I organize my time."

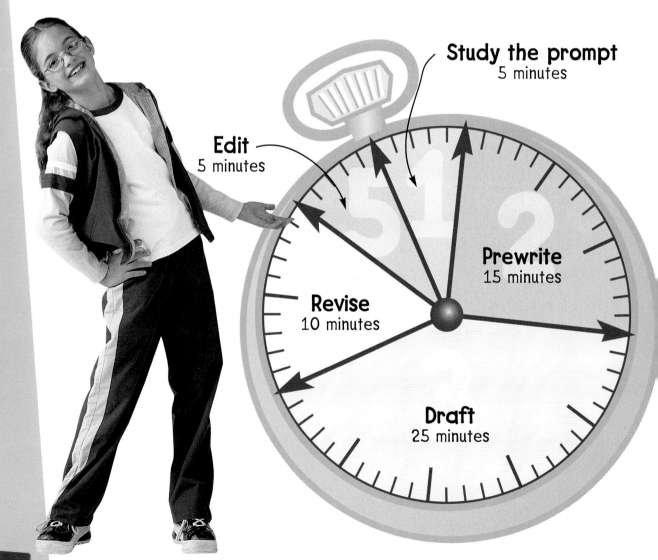

Study the prompt
5 minutes

Edit
5 minutes

Prewrite
15 minutes

Revise
10 minutes

Draft
25 minutes

Prewriting

Gather and Organize

Choose a graphic organizer. Use it to organize my ideas.

66 I don't have lots of time, so I'll gather ideas and organize them at the same time. First, I'll choose a useful graphic organizer. I'm writing a story, so a story map will help me organize the beginning, middle, and end. I can look back at page 161 to remind myself of how to use a story map. I'll also make notes on who the story is about and where and when the events take place. Some of the information comes directly from the Setup and Task parts of the writing prompt.

"We were asked to write a story about something that happened because of a special gift. What can I write about? I remember getting a very special gift from my grandmother. Something very special happened because of her nice gift. I'll write about that. Read my story map. 99

Setting
- **When?**   last fall
- **Where?**   at our soccer games

Characters
- Grammie, me, my team

Beginning
- I was always cold when I played soccer. (This is the problem.)
- Grammie started knitting special gifts to keep me warm.

Middle
- The team started winning.
- I played better when I was warm.
- Everyone else started wearing what she made.

End
- We won a special award at the finals.

Prewriting

Organize
Check my graphic organizer against the Scoring Guide.

> In a test, you don't always get much time to revise. Prewriting is more important than ever! So before I write, I'll check the information on my story map against the **Scoring Guide** in the writing prompt.

 Be sure your writing gets the audience's attention at the beginning and keeps it throughout the story.

> My story map tells what happens in the beginning of the story. I think the audience will wonder what type of gifts Grammie made for me. The events listed in the middle of my story map will keep my audience interested.

 Be sure your writing tells the events in the order they happen.

> I'll start by telling what happened at the beginning. If I tell what happened in order, it will be easier for my audience to follow the events in my story. I'll number the events on my story map, to help me write about them in order.
> "I'm in good shape. I'm ready to write!

Events
1. Grammie started knitting special gifts to keep me warm.
4. The team started winning.
2. I played better when I was warm.
3. Everyone else started wearing what she made.

Be sure your writing includes details to help the reader picture the characters and events.

"Hmm. I don't have any details yet, but that is okay. I'll add details when I write the story."

 Be sure your writing clearly tells who or what the story is about…

"That's in the characters part of my story map."

Characters
- Grammie, me, my team

 …and when and where it takes place.

"That's in the setting part of my story map."

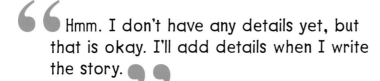

Setting
- **When?**   last fall
- **Where?** at our soccer games

 Be sure your writing uses the conventions of language and spelling correctly.

"That is something that I need to check later when I edit."

Go to page 127 in the **Practice** the Strategy **Notebook!**

Drafting

Write

Use my story map to write a good beginning, middle, and end.

“After I checked my story map one more time, here's what I wrote. I left room for corrections.”

Purple Panther Power Knitter   [DRAFT]

by Lucy

I'm sure Grammie didn't know what ~~would happen~~ she was getting into when she came to my first soccer game last fall. The Panthers lost, partly because of me. I was so cold. *(beginning)*

I sure was surprised when Grammie showed up at my practice the next day. She had a special gift for me. It was a pair of knee warmers. I put them on, and guess what? I was warm. I played much better that day.

We had a cold spell. Grammie kept her fingers warm though. She stayed busy making me more gifts. She made me a purple scarf and a purple nose warmer. Purple is the Panthers' team color. *(middle)*

The coach wouldn't let me wear the scarf. He thought it might be dangerous. Grammie decided to keep it for herself. She wore it to our games as she sat and cheered for us. In the meantime, all of the kids on my team begged for knee warmers and nose warmers of they own.

The funny thing is, when we war all that purple, we started winning. More and more people started coming to our games. grammie kept knitting. She showed other parents and grandparents how to knit. Grammie and her new buddies knitted scarves and sold them to the crowd. Pretty soon the Panthers and our fans was all covered in purple wool. Grammie even ~~did~~ knitted a sweater for my dog Sandy to where to the games!

middle

We did so well last season that ourselves got to go to the finals. The money from the scarves to pay for our trip. Our team didn't win, but we did get a special award it was for most team spirit. The team decided to give Grammie an award, too. Someone knitted a sweater with a purple panther on it. We pinned a ribbon on Grammies new sweater. It says "Purple Panther Power Knitter."

end

Be Neat!

" Remember, you may not get a chance to recopy your paper in a writing test. I try to be neat when I write. "

Go to page 128 in the **Practice** the Strategy **Notebook!**

Revising

Elaborate

Check what I have written against the Scoring Guide. Add any missing details.

> In a test, I can't read my paper to a partner, so I'll reread it to myself. I'll keep the **Scoring Guide** at hand so I can check my paper against it. For this test the **Scoring Guide** says that I need to add any missing details. I can add more details about why we lost the game and other details that will help readers picture what happened.

[DRAFT]

I'm sure Grammie didn't know what ~~would happen~~ she was

getting into when she came to my first soccer game last fall.
added detail ——→ shivering so much I couldn't kick straight
The Panthers lost, partly because of me. I was ~~so cold~~.

I sure was surprised when Grammie showed up at my

practice the next day. She had a special gift for me. It was
added ——→ purple   that she had knitted ←—— **added detail**
detail a pair of knee warmers. I put them on, and guess what?
                    and toasty ←—— **added detail**
I was warm. I played much better that day.

Go to page 130 in the **Practice** the Strategy **Notebook!**

Revising

Clarify
Check what I have written against the Scoring Guide. Make sure everything is clear.

" I'll read my paper again to make sure everything is clear. The **Scoring Guide** says that I need to let the reader know when and where the story takes place. I did say it happened last fall, but I think I can make this part a little clearer. "

READ TO MYSELF

[DRAFT]

when
for the next few days   during the games

We had a cold spell ∧. Grammie kept her fingers warm ∧
∧ in the stands ← where
though. She stayed busy ∧ making me more gifts. She made me

a purple scarf and a purple nose warmer. Purple is the

Panthers' team color.

while I was playing ← when
The coach wouldn't let me wear the scarf ∧. He thought it

might be dangerous.

Go to page 131 in the **Practice** the Strategy **Notebook!**

Editing

Proofread

Check that I have used correct grammar, capitalization, punctuation, and spelling.

" I always check my paper one last time. The **Scoring Guide** says to use correct grammar, capitalization, punctuation, and spelling. I always leave plenty of time to check for mistakes in these important areas.

"Using a checklist like this is a big help. We've used a list like the one below so often in our writing that I just about have it in my head. "

Conventions & Skills
Proofreading Checklist

- ☑ Do all the sentences have a subject and verb?
- ☑ Do the subjects and verbs agree?
- ☑ Does each sentence begin with a capital letter and end with the correct punctuation?
- ☑ Have compound sentences been joined with a comma and a joining word?
- ☑ Have homophones been used correctly?
- ☑ Have past-tense verbs been used correctly?
- ☑ Have pronouns been used correctly?
- ☑ Have adjectives that compare been used correctly?
- ☑ Do all proper nouns begin with a capital letter?
- ☑ Are all words spelled correctly?

Extra Practice
See **Review** (pages CS 22–CS 23) in the back of this book.

Proofreading Marks

⌐ Indent.

≡ Make a capital.

/ Make a small letter.

∧ Add something.

ℓ Take out something.

⊙ Add a period.

⌗ New paragraph

SP Spelling error

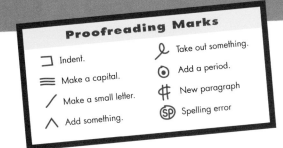

" When I proofread my work, I found a few errors and fixed them. It's a good thing I read my draft one more time! "

Purple Panther Power Knitter [DRAFT]

by Lucy

I'm sure Grammie didn't know what ~~would happen~~ she was

getting into when she came to my first soccer game last fall.

        shivering so much I couldn't kick straight

The Panthers lost, partly because of me. I was ~~so cold~~.
∧

I sure was surprised when Grammie showed up at my

practice the next day. She had a special gift for me. It was

      purple   that she had knitted

a pair of knee warmers . I put them on, and guess what?
    ∧ and toasty ∧

I was warm . I played much better that day.
      ∧   for the next few days   during the games

We had a cold spell . Grammie kept her fingers warm
         ∧ in the stands   ∧

though. She stayed busy making me more gifts. She made me
          ∧

a purple scarf and a purple nose warmer. Purple is the

Panthers' team color.

               while I was playing

The coach wouldn't let me wear the scarf . He thought it
                ∧

might be dangerous. Grammie decided to keep it for herself.

She wore it to our games as she sat and cheered for us. In

the meantime, all of the kids on my team begged for knee

            their

warmers and nose warmers of ~~they~~ own.
          ∧

The funny thing is, when we ~~wor~~ wore all that purple, we started winning. More and more people started coming to our games. ~~g~~Grammie kept knitting. She showed other parents and grandparents how to knit. Grammie and her new buddies knitted scarves and sold them to the crowd. Pretty soon the Panthers and our fans ~~was~~ were all covered in purple wool. Grammie even ~~did~~ knitted a sweater for my dog Sandy to ~~where~~ wear to the games!

We did so well last season that ~~ourselves~~ we got to go to the finals. We used The money from the scarves to pay for our trip. Our team didn't win, but we did get a special award⊙ it was for most team spirit. The team decided to give Grammie an award, too. Someone knitted a sweater with a purple panther on it. We pinned a ribbon on Grammie's new sweater. It says "Purple Panther Power Knitter."

Go to page 132 in the **Practice** the Strategy **Notebook!**

" We're finished! That wasn't so bad! The main thing to remember is that when you write for a test, you use the writing process. Remember these important tips when you write for a test. "

1. **Study the writing prompt before you start to write.**
   Remember, most writing prompts have three parts: the Setup, the Task, and the Scoring Guide. The parts will probably not be labeled. You need to remember what to do.

2. **Make sure you understand the task before you start to write.**
   - Read all three parts of the writing prompt carefully.
   - Circle key words in the Task part of the prompt that tell what kind of writing you need to do. The Task might also tell you who your audience is. If you don't know who the audience is, write for your teacher.
   - Make sure you know how you'll be graded.
   - Say what you need to do in your own words.

3. **Keep an eye on the clock.**
   Decide how much time you're going to spend on each part of the writing process and try to stick to it. Don't spend so much time on prewriting that you don't have any time left to write!

4. **Reread your writing. Check it against the Scoring Guide at least twice.**
   Remember the rubrics you've used all year? A Scoring Guide on a writing test is like a rubric. It can help you keep what's important in mind. That way you can make sure you've done everything the Scoring Guide asks you to do.

5. **Plan, plan, plan!**
   You don't get as much time or chance to revise during a test, so planning is more important than ever.

6. **Write neatly.**
   Remember, if the people who score your test can't read your writing, it doesn't matter how good your story is!

your own **TEST** writing

Narrative

Put the strategies you practiced in this unit to work. Use the writing prompt below to take your own narrative writing test. Pretend this is a real test and give yourself one hour to complete all of the steps. Use the **Scoring Guide** to evaluate your paper.

Think about a time you learned an important lesson. Write a story about what happened and what you learned. Be sure your writing

- gets the audience's attention at the beginning and keeps it throughout the story.
- tells the events in the order they happen.
- includes details to help your reader picture the characters and events.
- clearly tells who or what the story is about and when and where it takes place.
- uses the conventions of language and spelling correctly.

portfolio

School–Home Connection

Keep a writing portfolio. Think about adding the activities from the *Practice the Strategy Notebook* to your writing portfolio. You may want to take your portfolio home to share.

Conventions & SKiLLS

Do you need some more practice on the editing skills you worked with in this book? Use the activities in this section to get more practice. Complete each activity on a separate sheet of paper.

Table of Contents

A **sentence** is a group of words that tells a complete thought. The **subject** is the part of the sentence that tells whom or what the sentence is about. The subject can be one or more words. The **predicate** is the part of the sentence that tells what the subject is or does.

ReView the Rule

A sentence needs a subject and a predicate. A fragment is not a sentence, because it does not express a complete thought. A fragment is missing either a subject or a predicate.

Practice

Number your paper from 1.–24. Read each group of words. Decide if it is a sentence or a fragment. If it is a sentence, write **Correct** beside the number. If the words are a fragment, write **Subject** or **Predicate** to tell what is missing. Then rewrite the fragment as a complete sentence.

1. My Aunt Terry and Uncle Oko in Florida.
2. They invited me to visit them.
3. Live on a beach in Siesta Key.
4. Siesta Key is on the western coast.
5. Miles of beautiful white sandy beaches.
6. We walked for miles every morning.
7. Watched pelicans dive into the water.
8. They were catching fish.
9. Many interesting things washed ashore.
10. Dozens of clear shiny jellyfish.

11. I collected small brown seashells.

12. A group of students at a nature camp.

13. One day I found a bottle.

14. Washed up on the beach during the night.

15. Cloudy green glass and a screw top.

16. Thought it was empty at first.

17. Something was unusual about the bottle.

18. Brought it home and put it in a window.

19. Something was inside the bottle.

20. Worked very hard to unscrew the metal top.

21. Uncle Oko helped me.

22. A piece of paper lay folded inside.

23. Writer's name and address and a date.

24. The writer lived on nearby Sanibel Island.

Copy the following short paragraph on a separate sheet of paper.
Correct any sentence fragments.

One morning I saw something dark on the beach. Couldn't tell what it was at first. A large dark circle with a pointed tail. It was alive. Later learned it was a horseshoe crab. It certainly looked dangerous. Sharp spikes along part of its back. Horseshoe crabs are actually harmless. Have been around for millions of years. They have actually changed very little over the years.

A friendly letter is a way to share your thoughts and ideas with someone you know. To make your letters easy to read, they should include certain parts. These parts have **special punctuation**.

ReView the Rule

A friendly letter has five parts.

- The **heading** gives your address and the date. Use a comma to separate the city and state and another comma to separate the day and year.

- The **greeting** includes the name of the person you are writing to. It begins with a capital letter and ends with a comma.

- The **body** gives your message.

- The **closing** is a friendly way to say good-bye. It begins with a capital letter and ends with a comma.

- The **signature** is your name.

A letter's envelope has two parts:

- the **address** of the person receiving the letter

- the **return address** of the person sending the letter

Practice

Number a separate sheet of paper 1.–7. Read the letter and envelope on the next page. Write the name of each numbered part after each number.

[1.] 90 Roth Avenue
Hackensack, NJ 07601
January 13, 2003

[2.] Dear Terry,

[3.] What a storm we are having! The snow started yesterday and is still falling. I think we have at least two feet of snow. This must be a blizzard. Maybe they will call off school tomorrow! Do you have snow where you live? Write back soon.

[4.] Your cousin,

[5.] Pat

[6.] Pat Meeks
90 Roth Avenue
Hackensack, NJ 07601

[7.] Terry Griffin
6030 Seventh Avenue
Erie, PA 16504

This friendly letter is all mixed up. Rewrite it correctly. You can use Pat's letter above as a guide.

Yours truly, Erie, PA 16504 February 13, 2003 We always get a lot of snow because we are near Lake Erie. I like to go sledding and make snow forts. What do you like to do in the snow? 6030 Seventh Avenue, Dear Pat, Terry

A **sentence** is a group of words that tells one complete thought. There are four kinds of sentences. A sentence that tells something is a **statement**. A sentence that asks something is a **question**. A sentence that tells someone to do something is a **command**. A sentence that shows excitement or surprise is an **exclamation**.

ReView the Rule

Begin each sentence with a capital letter.
- Put a period (.) at the end of a statement and a command.
- Put a question mark (?) at the end of a question.
- Put an exclamation point (!) at the end of an exclamation.

Practice

Number your paper 1.–25. Read each sentence. Rewrite each incorrect sentence to correct any errors in capitalization or punctuation. If a sentence has no errors, write **Correct** after the number.

1. Trees can grow to be very large
2. people measure them in different ways.
3. Some trees can grow very tall.
4. California has many tall redwoods and sequoias
5. how can you tell them apart
6. redwoods have longer needles than sequoias.
7. look at this spot on the map.
8. Where do sequoias live
9. they grow in the mountains of California.
10. what a huge tree trunk that is

11. Big trees are measured in different places

12. what parts do people measure

13. Someone measured around that tree trunk

14. How old is that tree?

15. Some are thousands of years old

16. trees can be large in different ways.

17. one banyan tree in India covers three acres.

18. What an enormous tree

19. A banyan tree grows many different trunks

20. different kinds of trees reach different sizes.

21. What is the biggest tree?

22. That depends on what is measured

23. are you talking about height or weight?

24. Just try to weigh a tree

25. Scientists estimate the weight of living trees.

Copy the following paragraph on a separate sheet of paper. Correct
any mistakes.

The largest living thing is not a tree. It is not an animal? it is a
kind of mushroom. Most people call it a honey mushroom. How big
is it Well, one in Oregon is as large as 1665 football fields. this
one plant is more than three miles wide. Now that's big Do you
want to hear some even more surprising things The plant started
as a tiny cell. most of the plant is actually under the ground.

Compound Sentences

A simple sentence has one subject and one predicate and expresses a complete thought. Two simple sentences can be joined together with a joining word to make a **compound sentence**.

ReView the Rule

A compound sentence contains two complete thoughts. A compound sentence is made by joining two simple sentences with a joining word such as *and, but,* or *or.* A comma is used before the joining word.

Examples:

Yellowstone National Park has beautiful scenery, **and** it is home to many animals.

It is great in the summer, **but** it is also lovely in the winter.

You can hike in the park in the summer, **or** you can cross-country ski in the winter.

Practice

Number a separate sheet of paper 1.–20. Rewrite each pair of sentences below as one compound sentence. Don't forget to use a comma and a joining word. Underline the joining word.

1. Yellowstone National Park is huge. It has many visitors.

2. Most of the park is in Wyoming. Parts are in other states.

3. Visitors must be careful with campfires. Carelessness will ruin this great park.

4. The forests are beautiful. They can be dangerous.

5. Yellowstone has forest fires. Some last for days.

6. Fires can start naturally. People can start them, too.

7. Lightning strikes often. It seldom starts fires.

8. Fires need fuel. The forests provide this.

9. Fuel might be pine needles. It could be entire trees.

10. Some forests are young. They have little that burns.

11. Older forests have dead trees. They also have shrubs.

12. A campfire may appear to be out. Hours later the ashes may reignite.

13. Trees are wet in the winter. They do not burn well.

14. Forests are dry in the summer. The risk of fire is high.

15. Dry weather helps fires form winds. These winds spread the fire.

16. Fire can kill trees. It can also help them.

17. Yellowstone has many lodgepole pines. These are special trees.

18. They have sticky cones. Their seeds are sealed inside.

19. Heat opens the cones. The seeds fall out.

20. The seeds drop. New trees begin.

Apply

Copy the following short paragraph on a separate sheet of paper. Correct any errors in forming compound sentences.

Dark clouds of smoke filled the sky walls of flame formed below them. A firefighting airplane flew overhead it could not really be heard. The crackle of the flames was too loud. The plane carried water it might have been carrying smokejumpers. These firefighters parachute into forest fires. They have a hard job everyone appreciates them. Everyone wanted to keep the fire from spreading the firefighters put it out.

Homophones

Words that sound the same are not a problem when we speak. When you say "Is this your hat?" or "You're wearing my hat," the meaning is clear. When you write, however, you must choose the correct spelling. The wrong spelling will confuse your reader.

ReView the Rule

Some words sound the same but are spelled differently and have different meanings. These words are called **homophones**.

- *Your* means "belonging to you." *You're* is a contraction that means "you are."
- *Their* means "belonging to them." *They're* is a contraction that means "they are." *There* means "at or in that place."
- *Its* means "belonging to it." *It's* is a contraction that means "it is" or "it has."

Practice

Number a separate piece of paper from 1.–24. Then write the word in ( ) that correctly completes each sentence.

1. If (your/you're) going camping, bring a flashlight.
2. Don't forget (its/it's) batteries.
3. Is (their/they're/there) a campground nearby?
4. The counselor said (their/they're/there) planning to leave early.
5. Have you seen (their/they're/there) map of the forest?
6. Did you remember (your/you're) tent ropes?
7. I know (your/you're) going to enjoy this trip.
8. How will we know when (its/it's) time to leave?
9. I think (their/they're/there) about to call us.

10. You will need (your/you're) blanket to stay warm tonight.

11. It is colder (their/they're/there) than you think.

12. Hikers who forget to bring (their/they're/there) water will be sorry.

13. (Its/It's) a long hike to the campground.

14. Find a nice, clear place to put up (your/you're) tent.

15. Hold the large tent by (its/it's) edges.

16. The rangers said we could use (their/they're/there) firewood.

17. Do you think (its/it's) too early to build a fire?

18. Be sure to put (your/you're) food away, or the bears will eat it.

19. Carry the heavy cooking pot by (its/it's) handles.

20. Place rocks tightly around (your/you're) campfire.

21. Most of the campers say (their/they're/there) going to bed soon.

22. Put your cell phone (their/they're/there) on the stump.

23. I'm glad (your/you're) television works on batteries.

24. (Its/It's) sure nice to get away from it all!

Copy the following short paragraph on your own sheet of paper. Correct any homophones that are used incorrectly.

> Your going to love Sagatuck Forest. I think you should go their for a few days. You will find it's the perfect place to relax. You can bike along it's many paths or just sit and read you're favorite book. All my friends say there going back again next year. It's one of my favorite places.

Verbs describe the action of a noun. They also tell when the action takes place. A **past-tense verb** tells about action that happened in the past.

ReView the Rule

Past-tense verbs show that the action happened in the past. Many past-tense verbs end in *-ed*.

Some verbs do not add *-ed* to form the past tense. They have different forms. Here are the past-tense forms of some of these irregular verbs:

Present Tense	Past Tense	With *have, has,* or *had*
sing(s)	sang	sung
bring(s)	brought	brought
ring(s)	rang	rung
go(es)	went	gone
come(s)	came	come
give(s)	gave	given
take(s)	took	taken
eat(s)	ate	eaten
sleep(s)	slept	slept

Examples:
 I **sing** in the school choir.
 I **sang** in the school choir last year.
 I **have sung** in the school choir for three years.

Practice

Number a separate sheet of paper 1.–15. Write the word in ( ) that correctly completes each sentence.

  1. Last year my sister and I (took/taked) a trip to the mountains.

  2. We both (wanted/wants) to learn to ski.

3. I had not (sleeped/slept) well because I was so excited.

4. I (wants/wanted) someone to teach me to ski.

5. I soon (learn/learned) how to put on my skis.

6. Later in the morning we (taked/took) a ride on the ski lift.

7. The ride (gave/given) me a wonderful view of the mountains.

8. I (look/looked) at the trees and the snow-covered peaks.

9. Little by little we (climbs/climbed) up the mountain.

10. I closed my eyes and (sang/singed) a little song.

11. At the top of the mountain everyone (jump/jumped) off the lift.

12. I had (closed/closes) my eyes, and I forgot where I was.

13. Suddenly my chair (turn/turned), and I was going down the mountain.

14. While others (skis/skied) down the mountain, I rode down.

15. I really (enjoys/enjoyed) the view, but I didn't get to ski down that time.

Rewrite the following paragraph. Change each verb that is incorrect so that it correctly tells about the past.

We comed home from the resort on Saturday afternoon. The next day I gone to Nana's house. She stay home when we goed to the mountains. I give her a picture of me. A friend take it when I rode the ski lift. I bringed Nana a box of candy. We eat and talk about my trip to the mountains. Later, we go to a store to buy a frame for Nana's new picture.

Subject and Object Pronouns

A **pronoun** is a word that can take the place of one or more nouns. A **subject pronoun** can take the place of a noun in the subject of a sentence. An **object pronoun** can come after action verbs and words such as *to, at, for, of,* and *with*.

ReView the Rule

Use the pronouns *I, you, he, she, it, we,* and *they* if the pronouns take the place of nouns in the subject. Use the pronouns *me, you, him, her, it, us,* and *them* as objects of action verbs or after words such as *to, at, for, of,* or *with*.

Practice

Number your paper 1.–20. Write a pronoun that could take the place of the underlined word or words in each sentence. Remember to capitalize the first word of a sentence.

1. "The students and I have several new students," said Ms. Wu.
2. Then Ms. Wu mentioned Mike, Tamara, and Ester.
3. She asked the rest of the class and me for a favor.
4. "The new students will need some help," Ms. Wu added.
5. "The students in the class can help Mike, Tamara, and Ester learn everyone's names," she told us.
6. "Ms. Wu will help, too," said Ms. Wu.
7. Tamara knew one girl in the class.
8. Tamara knew that girl from camp.
9. Tamara said, "You sat next to Tamara on the field trip."
10. Ms. Wu made Ester the class messenger.

11. Messengers collect lunch money. People give <u>lunch money</u> to them.

12. The people must give their names to <u>the messengers</u>.

13. Soon <u>Ester</u> knew the names of twelve students.

14. Ms. Wu looked at <u>Mike</u> thoughtfully.

15. Later, <u>Mike</u> found an envelope on his desk.

16. He opened <u>the envelope</u> after school.

17. "Soon you will know all of <u>the students</u>," said the note.

18. "Until then, <u>you and I</u> will be secret friends."

19. "In school tomorrow, smile at <u>the writer of this note</u>," said the note.

20. At school the next day, Mike smiled at everyone who looked at <u>Mike</u>.

Read this part of a story. Rewrite the paragraph on a separate sheet of paper, correcting any pronoun errors that you find.

> For days, Mike wondered about the note. Who was this secret friend? Him tried to guess. The writer might be Jenna. She was always nice to him. Sometimes she helped he find things or people. Once, he got lost on the way to the library. Jenna led him to it. Mike also wondered about the Abbott twins. Maybe them sent the note. On Friday, one spoke to him before class. "Jerry and me will sit with you at lunch today."
> Mike was glad that him had many new friends.

An **adjective** describes, or tells about, a noun. An adjective can describe by comparing two persons, places, or things. An adjective can also compare more than two persons, places, or things.

ReView the Rule

Add *-er* to most short adjectives to compare two things. Use *smoother* instead of *more smooth*. For most longer adjectives, use the word *more* before the adjective. Use *more wonderful* instead of *wonderfuler*.

Add *-est* to short adjectives to compare more than two things. Use *smallest* instead of *most small*. For most longer adjectives, use the word *most* before the adjective. Use *most beautiful* instead of *beautifulest*.

If the adjective ends in *y*, remember to change the *y* to *i* before adding the ending.

Practice

Number your paper 1.–18. Rewrite each sentence. Write the word or words in ( ) to complete each sentence correctly.

1. Fables and folktales are some of the (older/oldest) stories around.

2. A fable is often (shorter/shortest) than a folktale.

3. In some fables, two animals argue over who is (smarter/smartest).

4. A wise character usually ends up (happier/happiest) than a foolish one.

5. The (smaller/smallest) fable character I know is an ant.

6. In that fable, the grasshopper is (more cheerful/cheerfuler) than the ant.

7. However, he is (lazier/laziest) than the ant.

8. Older animals are usually the (most intelligent/intelligenter).

9. Aesop is probably the (famousest/most famous) teller of fables.

10. Oftentimes in fables, a helpless animal, like a mouse, turns out to be (wiser/wisest).

11. In fables, a small animal is usually (more intelligent/intelligenter) than a large one.

12. One of the (most funny/funniest) fables is about a rabbit and a turtle.

13. Everyone knows a rabbit can run (faster/fastest) than a turtle.

14. Rabbit wanted to prove he was the (faster/fastest) animal in the forest.

15. Beating Turtle in a race would be the (easier/easiest) thing he had ever done.

16. However, Rabbit was also the (lazier/laziest) animal in the forest.

17. Turtle knew it was (more smart/smarter) to keep moving than to rest.

18. As Rabbit rested, the (slower/slowest) animal won the race.

Copy the following short paragraphs. Correct any adjectives that are used incorrectly.

One day Dog, Horse, and Flea began arguing. Which one of them was the most fast? They decided to have a contest. Whoever could swim across the river first would be the fastest.

Rain had fallen, so the river was deeper and more wide than usual. Dog was certain that he would win. Horse was even certainer that he would win. Flea, however, quietly made a plan. First, Flea bit Horse, who then stopped to scratch. Then Flea jumped on Dog's back as Dog swam across the river. When Dog got near the other side, Flea flew to shore ahead of Dog. Even though he was the smaller animal, he won.

Proper Nouns

There are two types of nouns: common nouns and proper nouns. A common noun names a person, place, or thing. The words *girl, city,* and *building* are common nouns. A **proper noun** names a particular, or specific, person, place or thing. The words *Margaret, Springfield,* and *Empire State Building* are proper nouns. The first letter in each proper noun is capitalized.

ReView the Rule

Proper nouns are the names of particular, or specific, people, places, or things.
- Capitalize a person's first and last name.
- Capitalize each important word in the names of streets, towns, countries, parks, lakes, rivers, oceans, and mountains.

Practice

Number a separate sheet of paper 1.–24. Rewrite each sentence that has an error. Correct any errors in the capitalization of proper nouns. If there are no errors, write **Correct**.

1. Last week our teacher, Mrs. clark, gave us some homework.
2. We were to go to maplewood memorial library.
3. This big library is at the corner of main street and Bay Street.
4. Mrs. Clark said to ask the librarian to help us make a list of celebrations held in the united states.
5. Everyone knows about Thanksgiving Day and independence day.
6. However, did you know about delaware Day?
7. It celebrates the day the first state approved the constitution.
8. In oklahoma, november 4 is Will rogers Day, a day named for the famous actor and humorist.
9. The birthday of Susan B. anthony is a holiday in parts of florida.

10. Many states celebrate arbor day by planting trees.

11. In my town we meet in memorial park.

12. There we are given seeds and tiny maple trees to plant in our yard.

13. Did you know that one state celebrates andrew jackson's birthday?

14. Many interesting celebrations take place in april.

15. This is the month when the Minutemen fired the shot heard round the world.

16. It is also the month when texans remember sam houston's victory at San jacinto.

17. The librarian, Ms. harper, was very helpful.

18. She told us about another special day in january.

19. Some schools celebrate benjamin franklin's birthday on January 17.

20. This american patriot was also an inventor and printer.

21. He once said that a penny saved is a penny earned.

22. At Alcott elementary school, Franklin's birthday is the start of Thrift Week.

23. Students all go to first community bank and open savings accounts.

24. That is a great idea, and we can't wait to tell Mrs. Clark about it on monday.

Apply

Rewrite the following paragraph on a separate sheet of paper. Correct any errors you find in the capitalization of proper nouns.

A great celebration takes place in boston on the third monday in april. It is called patriots' day. It recalls the battle of lexington and concord, the event that started the revolutionary war. People gather at the old battlefield. There they watch men and women in costumes perform the battle. Later, hundreds of runners race in the boston marathon. It is a grand sight to see!

Every sentence must have a **subject** and a **verb**. It is important for the subject of a sentence to agree with the verb. You must sometimes add an ending to a verb, or replace it, for it to agree with its subject.

ReView the Rule

Follow these rules for subject-verb agreement:
- Add *-s* or *-es* to a regular verb in the present tense when the subject is a singular noun or *he, she,* or *it.*
- Do not add *-s* or *-es* to a regular verb in the present tense when the subject is a plural noun or *I, you, we,* or *they.*
- Use *is* or *was* after a singular subject.
- Use *are* or *were* after a plural subject.

Practice

Number a separate sheet of paper 1.–24. Write the subject of the sentence and the verb in ( ) that correctly completes it.

1. Many children (is/are) active in sports.
2. Soccer (is/are) one of the most popular sports.
3. Players (need/needs) little equipment to get started.
4. Two nets (stand/stands) at the end of a flat field.
5. A soccer ball (is/are) about 27 inches around.
6. It (weigh/weighs) about 15 ounces.
7. Players (wear/wears) special shoes and leg guards.
8. A player (kick/kicks) the ball.
9. He (hit/hits) the ball with his head or body.
10. A player called a goalie (guard/guards) the net.

11. Goalies may (touch/touches) the ball with their hands.

12. Other players cannot (touch/touches) the ball at any time.

13. Nearly every country (play/plays) the game of soccer.

14. Soccer (was/were) played in ancient China.

15. England (was/were) the birthplace of the modern game.

16. Soccer (is/are) an important part of the Summer Olympics.

17. Soccer (was/were) included for the first time in the 1900 Olympic Games.

18. Many nations (compete/competes) for the World Cup.

19. Over a billion people (watch/watches) this game on television.

20. Pelé (was/were) the most famous athlete in the world in 1975.

21. He (is/are) best known for leading Brazil to three World Cups.

22. Thousands of boys and girls in the United States now (enjoy/enjoys) playing soccer.

23. Professional teams (exist/exists) in many American cities.

24. The many leagues for boys and girls now (offer/offers) everyone a chance to play.

Below are some headlines from the sports page of a newspaper. Copy each headline. Correct any errors in subject-verb agreement you find.

Pelé Score Winning Goal

Brazil Takes the World Cup

Scoring Record Were Broken

Spectators Cheers the Winning Goal

American Team Are Victorious

Hundreds Watch Game on TV

Proofreading Checklist

☑ Do all the sentences have a subject and verb?

☑ Do the subjects and verbs agree?

☑ Does each sentence begin with a capital letter and end with the correct punctuation?

☑ Have compound sentences been joined with a comma and a joining word?

☑ Have homophones been used correctly?

☑ Have past-tense verbs been used correctly?

☑ Have pronouns been used correctly?

☑ Have adjectives that compare been used correctly?

☑ Do all proper nouns begin with a capital letter?

☑ Are all words spelled correctly?

Practice

Number your paper 1.–25. Rewrite each sentence. Correct any errors in grammar, capitalization, punctuation, and spelling. If a sentence has no errors, write **Correct**. Use the checklist above to help you.

1. Everyone says i am a great soccer player.

2. Our team wins most games

3. Taught me how to play.

4. I hope your coming to my next game.

5. Will the game be played here.

6. It will be played at jones park.

7. Our team arrives the most early of all the teams, and we practice for an hour.

8. Our coach watch us do our drills.

9. Everyone bringed warm socks.

10. It was a cold day but I soon forgot about the weather.

11. My parents comed to every game last year.

12. How exciting it was?

13. June and me are the captains of the team.

14. Is'nt soccer a great game!

15. Their are several important rules in soccer.

16. It's against the rules to pick up the ball.

17. Tripping another player.

18. The goalie guards the net and she is allowed to pick up the ball.

19. The referee blow the whistle to start the game.

20. Ruth taked a pass from Yum.

21. She kicked the ball to Tess and I.

22. The ball goed into the goal.

23. What a great feeling that was?

24. We heard my parents cheering for us.

25. Its always fun to play.

Write the following newspaper article. Correct any mistakes.

Dodgeville Panthers Win Close Game

The dodgeville Panthers tooked an early lead in monday's game and they never gave it up. Coach west said cold weather isnt a problem for the Panthers. in fact they seem to luv it. She said that Yum Kim and Ruth brown were the keys to the win. There possibly the best players in the league.

Writer's HandBook

Writer's Handbook

The Writer's Handbook is designed to give you more help as well as some great hints for making your writing the best it can be. It uses the Gather, Organize, Write, Elaborate, Clarify, Proofread, and Share categories you have become familiar with during the course of this book. Use the Writer's Handbook any time you have more questions or just need a little extra help.

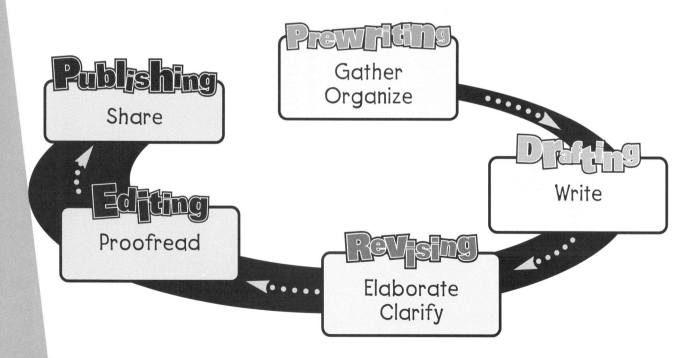

Table of Contents

Research

Research is an important part of writing. When you look for information about a topic, you are doing research. It's important to use good sources.

A **source** is anything or anyone with information. **Primary sources** include books or people that are closest to the information. Diaries, journals, and other writings of people who lived during the described events are considered primary sources. **Secondary sources** are books or people who use other books or people to get information. Primary and secondary sources fit into three categories—**printed, electronic,** and **personal**.

Use a variety of primary and secondary sources from different categories when you do research. That way you can make sure the information is accurate, and you will have lots of it to choose from. Talk to your teacher about how many sources and what kinds of sources to use for different writing projects.

- **Printed sources** include books, magazines, newspapers, letters, journals and diaries, and reference materials such as encyclopedias and dictionaries.

- **Electronic sources** include the Internet, television, radio, and videos.

- **Personal sources** include people you interview or observe and your own experiences and memories.

When doing research, keep these points in mind:

- When you use sources, be sure they are **credible** ones. Credible means that the source can be trusted to have accurate information. Generally, books, magazines, and reference materials can be considered credible sources. People who are experts in their field and those you know and trust personally are also credible sources.

- Use caution when using Web sites, movies, and television as sources. Many Web sites offer the opinion of the people who created them, not necessarily the facts about a topic. Check several Web sites and some printed sources on the same topic to be sure you are getting "just the facts." Also, Web sites often move or become outdated, so check to see that the ones you are using are still in operation. Finally, make sure you have an adult—a teacher or parent—help you as you do research on the Internet.

- Movies and television offer a lot of information, but it is often difficult to tell if the information is fact, fiction, or someone's opinion. Again, double check with other sources and with an adult to be sure you are getting accurate information.

Printed

Sources

Books, Magazines,
Newspapers, Reference Materials,
Letters, Journals/Diaries

Where to Find Them

Library, Home,
School,
Bookstores,
Discount Department Stores

How to Use Them

Use headings to find useful information.
Read.
Take notes while reading.

How to Cite Them

(Use punctuation and capitalization as shown.)

Books: Author's Last Name, First Name. Book Title. City: Publishing Company, year.

Magazine Articles: Author's Last Name, First Name. "Title of Article." Title of Magazine, volume number (if there is one), date, month, or season, and year of publication: page number. (If the article is longer than one page, state the first page and the last page of the article with a dash between them.)

Encyclopedias/Dictionaries: Title of Encyclopedia or Dictionary, edition number (ed. ___), s.v. "item." (If you looked up Olympic Games, it would be s.v. "Olympic Games.")

Letters/Diaries/Journals: Mention them in the text as you are writing, rather than citing them later.

Electronic

The Internet,
Television,
Radio,
Videos

The Internet,
Television,
Radio,
Stores, Library

Read Web sites.
Watch the news on television.
Listen to radio programs.
Rent or check out videos.
Take notes as you are reading,
watching, and listening.

Internet: State the Web address
of the Web sites you used. Most
Web addresses will begin with
http:// and end with .com, .net,
.org, or .edu.

Films/Videos: Title of Film or
Video. City where the production
company is located: Production
Company Name, year.

Television/Radio: Mention them
in the text as you are writing,
rather than citing them later.

Personal

Self,
Other People

Home: Parents, Siblings,
Grandparents
School: Teachers, Principals,
Librarians, Friends, Other Family
Members, People in the Community

Listen to people when they tell
stories.
Interview people who know
something about your topic.
Ask questions.
Take notes.

Personal sources should be
mentioned in the text as you are
writing.
When interviewing, you can
quote the person by enclosing his
or her exact words in quotation
marks. You can also use phrases
such as "according to" to give
credit to your source.
To give credit to personal sources
other than people you interview,
simply state where you found the
information.

Getting Ideas for Writing

So you have a writing assignment. Now what? Where do you begin? Your mind might be a complete blank right now. You haven't even chosen a topic yet. The early stages of writing are the toughest ones. Good writers use all kinds of techniques to generate new ideas. Here are some to help you get started.

Brainstorming

Brainstorming is a great way to generate lots of ideas in a short amount of time. You can brainstorm alone or with a group of people. All you have to do is say or think one word, and you're off! Here's how it works:

Your assignment is to write an expository essay about an animal. If you're working in a group, the members of the group can brainstorm together. One person starts by saying "animals." The rest of the group can now take turns saying words or phrases that come to mind. Someone says "mammals." Someone else says "reptiles." Another person says "dinosaurs." As this is happening, members of the group should be careful to take turns and give each other time to write down what's being said. As the process continues, you or someone else in the group will probably say something that will become the topic for your essay.

If you're working alone, the process is the same. Think of the initial assignment. Write down words related to the assignment as they come to mind. Eventually, you will find the one word or phrase that will become the topic for your essay. Remember to write down your thoughts as you brainstorm alone, too. That way, if you change your mind, you'll have other choices.

Journaling

A journal is similar to a diary. Both are used to write down personal thoughts. However, diaries are usually used to record daily events and feelings. Journals are generally used to record thoughts, impressions, and responses to events. A journal is a great way to generate ideas for writing.

Writers who use journals keep one with them most of the time. You might want to keep your journal in your book bag or locker and take it home with you after school. That way, when an interesting thought occurs to you, you can write it in your journal no matter where you are. The great thing about journaling is that there's no right or wrong way to do it. It's also great because you don't have to try to keep every good idea in your head. Just write it down and it will always be there, ready to become a topic for writing.

Freewriting

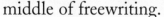

Freewriting is a very unusual method of writing because it has no form. The idea behind freewriting is to write down everything that comes to mind during a specific period of time. Just get out a piece of paper and a pen or pencil, or sit down in front of a computer. For the next few minutes, jot down everything your mind comes up with, even stuff that doesn't make any sense. You don't have to use complete sentences. You don't have to worry about spelling. You don't even have to write words. You can draw, sketch, or doodle as part of freewriting.

When time is up, stop writing (or doodling) and look at what you've got. Read it over a couple of times. You'll be amazed at what you might find. Some of the best ideas for writing show up in the middle of freewriting.

Daydreaming

This one is best done at home. Your teachers probably won't appreciate your daydreaming during class, and daydreaming while crossing the road is downright dangerous.

Try this. When you have some free time at home, get a mug of something good to drink (hot chocolate works great on a cold day). Now find a comfortable spot and—are you ready for this?—don't do anything! At least, don't do anything specific. Daydreaming means letting your mind wander wherever it wants to go. Stare out the window. Watch the goldfish in your fish tank. Listen to the rain. Smell dinner cooking in the kitchen. Think about what you'll be when you're an adult. Something will probably come to mind that will make a great topic for writing.

Here's a tip for how to use daydreaming. As soon as you hit upon a great topic for writing, get up and write down everything you can think of before you forget it. You can organize it later, but it's very important to record it all now. Just like dreams you dream at night, daydreams will disappear quickly, and you don't want to lose all those great ideas.

Reading

Sometimes the easiest way to get ideas for writing is to read. For example, let's say you have been asked to write a piece of narrative historical fiction. You don't know much about history. How do you write about something you don't know? Make use of your library.

Talk to your school librarian or go to the public library and ask for help at the information desk. These people are experts. Tell them you are looking for a few books about history. They will probably ask you some questions such as, "What kind of history are you interested in reading about?" or, "Would you like books about U.S. history or world history?" These questions will help you to make some early decisions about your writing. Once you decide what kind of history you want to read about, pick a few books that are short enough to read quickly, but long enough to have lots of interesting information. Again, people who work at libraries can help you through this process.

As you read about history, you will spot things that interest you. Write down those things. Skip over the stuff you don't find interesting, at least for now. When you are finished reading, look at the notes you took. Do they have anything in common? Do most of them have something to do with specific time periods, people, or things in history? For example, in reading about U.S. history, did you always stop at the sections about inventions because you found that information interesting? Maybe you can focus your writing assignment on an invention or an inventor.

Don't forget to read for your own interest and pleasure. The more you read, the more you'll know. The more you know, the more ideas for writing you will have.

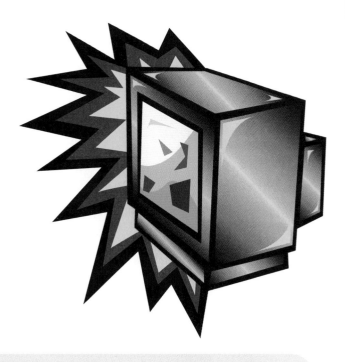

TV/Movies

Great ideas for writing may be as close as your television or movie theater. There are cable channels that run programs specifically about science, technology, history, animals, cooking, music, sports, and just about any other topic you can think of. Public television also has great documentaries and programs about interesting and unusual topics.

Movies can also be good for generating ideas for writing—especially movies that deal with specific topics. Are you a fan of sci-fi movies? You can use your favorite sci-fi movie to come up with ideas for an expository essay about artificial intelligence or a compare-and-contrast report about robots and computers.

Just as you should use caution when using television and movies as sources when you write, be cautious in using them to generate ideas. Make sure you talk to an adult about appropriate and safe choices in movies and television programs.

Interviewing

An interview is the process of asking questions of another person and listening to and recording that person's answers. Interviews make good sources for writing projects, especially if the person you interview is an expert about your topic. Interviews can also be good ways to generate ideas for writing.

Some of the most interesting stories come from people in your community and family. Your parents and grandparents have lived through many events. Sit down with a family member or another trusted adult and ask that person to tell you about a memorable event he or she experienced or an interesting person he or she knew. You'll be amazed at the stories you will hear. Many famous authors say that their stories were inspired by what other people have told them.

As you listen to people's stories, jot down notes. It's safe to say that something the person said during the interview will probably give you a good idea for your own writing project.

Note Taking

As you are doing research for your writing project, you will want to take notes. That way you will have the most important information in small pieces that you can use easily. However, taking notes can be tricky, especially for the beginner. Here are some things to keep in mind:

- Keep your notes short. You don't have to use complete sentences, as long as you include the important information.

- Make sure your handwriting is legible. If you scribble, you may not be able to read your own notes later.

- Use note cards. That way you can arrange your notes without having to rewrite them. Try using different colors of note cards to help you organize your notes.

- When listening to a speaker and taking notes, don't try to write down what the speaker is saying "word for word." Just make sure you get the important stuff.

- When you are interviewing, however, you will want to get the exact words down on paper. In this case, ask the speaker to repeat what he or she said, so you can write the quote. If it's possible, use a tape recorder during the interview, so you can listen to the quote as often as you need to. Just make sure you get the speaker's permission to record the interview.

- It's important to write down the source of your information on your note cards as you are taking notes. That way you can cite or credit your sources easily.

Graphic Organizers

A graphic organizer is a tool that helps writers put information in order before they start a draft. In this book, you have practiced working with lots of graphic organizers. You have worked with webs, spider maps, attribute charts, character charts, story maps, and other kinds of graphic organizers. When you do other writing projects, you'll want to continue to use them to help you keep track of information. What kind of graphic organizers you use depends on what kind of writing project you have. Check back with this book to see what kind of graphic organizer works best for different writing projects.

Outlining

There are many ways to organize information. One very useful organizer is an outline.

The outline helps you put your information in the order it will appear in your writing. The outline can be divided into several basic pieces—the introduction, the body, and the conclusion—just like a basic essay. Every letter and number in the outline stands for something in your essay. Words or phrases that are shown with Roman numerals represent entire chunks of an essay. Words or phrases that are shown with capital letters represent paragraphs, which support a main statement or idea.

You can use an outline to organize almost any kind of writing—from expository essays to science fiction stories. It will help you make sure that every piece of information has a place and is used in the best way possible.

I. Introduction

gets audience's attention ——→ **A. Lead**

moves closer to the main idea ——→ **B. Related statement**

states main idea of essay ——→ **C. Transitional statement**

introduce the essay to the audience

II. Body

states main idea of paragraph ——→ **A. First main idea**

    1. First supporting detail

    2. Second supporting detail

    3. Third supporting detail

support, explain, and give more information about main idea of essay

  B. Second main idea

    1. First supporting detail

    2. Second supporting detail

    3. Third supporting detail

same as paragraph A

  C. Third main idea

    1. First supporting detail

    2. Second supporting detail

    3. Third supporting detail

same as paragraphs A and B

III. Conclusion

restates main ideas of body paragraphs ——→ **A. Brief summary of main ideas**

begins to wrap up essay ——→ **B. Other related statement**

ends the essay ——→ **C. Closing statement**

wrap up essay

Drafting Write

Writing Paragraphs

A paragraph is a group of related sentences. In other words, every sentence in a paragraph should be about the same main idea. The main idea of a paragraph is usually in the first sentence, called the **topic sentence**. The rest of the sentences in a paragraph give more information about the topic sentence. The additional information can be examples, details, or supporting statements for the main idea.

How do you write a good paragraph? Start with the idea you want your audience to know. Write that idea in the form of a sentence. This will become the topic sentence for your paragraph. For example, let's say your essay is an expository piece about apples. You have gathered information about apples and made a graphic organizer to put your information in order.

Your graphic organizer may look something like this:

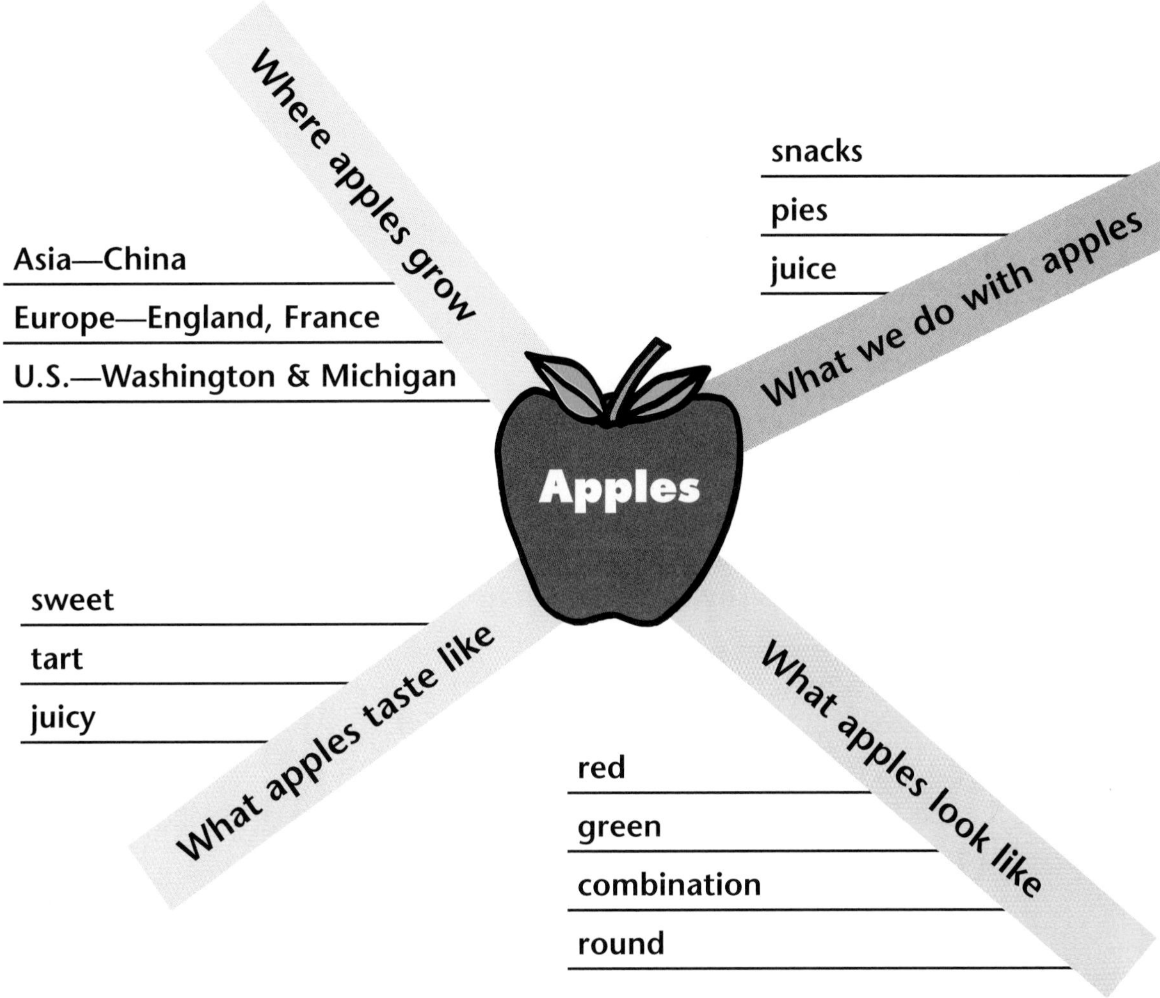

Where apples grow

Asia—China

Europe—England, France

U.S.—Washington & Michigan

What we do with apples

snacks

pies

juice

Apples

What apples taste like

sweet

tart

juicy

What apples look like

red

green

combination

round

Take one part of the graphic organizer—where apples grow. Write it as a sentence. You might come up with this:

Apples grow on trees all over the world.

This is now your topic sentence. Now it's time to tell your audience more information about it. Use the details in your graphic organizer to write some supporting sentences.

1. In the United States, apples grow in several states, including Washington and Michigan.

2. England, France, and other European countries also have apple trees.

3. In Asia, apples grow in China.

When you combine your topic sentence with these supporting sentences, you have a paragraph.

Apples grow on trees all over the world. In the United States, apples grow in several states, including Washington and Michigan. England, France, and other European countries also have apple trees. In Asia, apples grow in China.

Following the same steps for the other three parts of your graphic organizer will give you three more paragraphs. Put these together, and you will have the body of a well-organized essay. All you need now is an introduction and a conclusion. For tips about writing good introductions and conclusions, see "Writing a Five-Paragraph Essay" on page HB 22.

Writing a Five-Paragraph Essay

An essay is a piece of nonfiction writing about one topic. In grades 3 and 4, you practice writing a compare-and-contrast essay, a how-to essay, and a persuasive essay. Essays are made up of three basic parts: the introduction, the body, and the conclusion.

Write the body of your essay first. It doesn't matter that you don't have an introduction yet. It's very difficult to write a good introduction until you have written the body. Imagine trying to introduce a person you don't know to an audience. What would you say? That's kind of what it's like to try writing an introduction first. You don't know your essay yet. Write the body first and then you'll know what to say in your introduction.

Body

The body of your essay is where you explain, describe, prove, and give information about your main idea. Look at your graphic organizer. There's a good chance that you already have the makings of several good paragraphs.

Let's pretend you're writing a persuasive essay on why cats make the best pets. After gathering and organizing your information, you may have three main points about cats in your graphic organizer—easy to take care of, good with children, and smart. Look at the web on page HB 23.

To move from one paragraph to the next, use a trick good writers know. It's called a "signal word." There's a list of these words on page HB 39.

Once you have written all the paragraphs of the body of your essay, it's time to write the introduction and the conclusion.

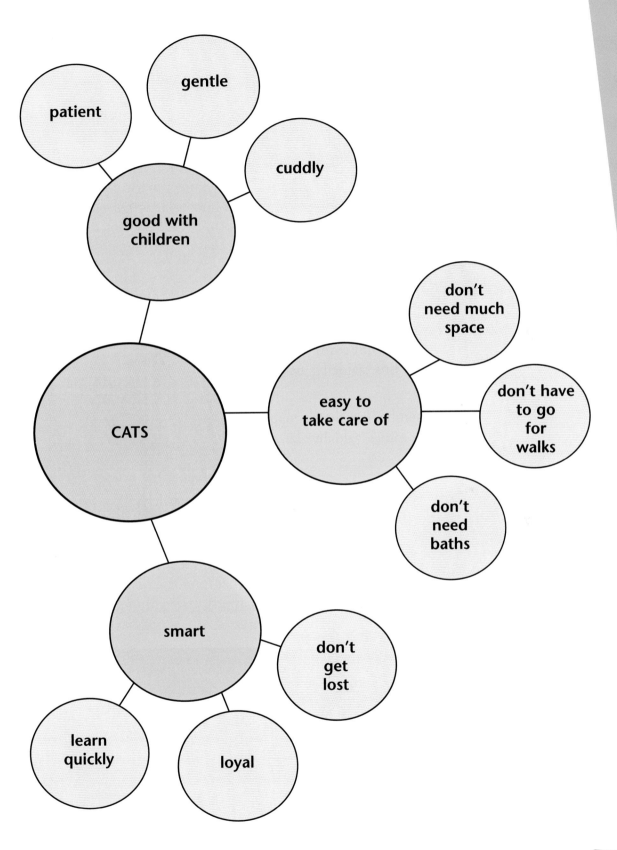

Introduction

The introduction is the first part of the essay that your audience will read or hear. You want it to get their attention and make them interested enough to keep reading or listening. What you don't want to do is give away what's in the essay. If you do, your audience will have no reason to keep reading or listening.

The Upside-Down Pyramid

If your introduction were a graphic organizer, it would look like an upside-down pyramid, with more general information at the beginning and more specific information at the end. Let's write an introduction for our essay about why cats make the best pets.

The first sentence of your introduction should say something true but general about your topic.

Many people like to keep pets.

This sentence introduces the idea of cats as pets. It's still true and still pretty general.

Cats are popular pets all over the world.

This sentence should be the main idea of your essay.

For many reasons, cats make the best pets.

Here's the complete introduction:

Many people like to keep pets. Cats are popular pets all over the world. For many reasons, cats make the best pets.

Remember—start with something general and true. Then say something a little more specific. Finish with the main idea of the essay. Now your introduction is complete.

Conclusion

The conclusion of an essay does two things. It restates the main idea of the essay, and it wraps up the essay. Restating the main idea is important. You want to make sure your audience remembers what the essay was about. Wrapping things up helps the audience feel that they have read a complete work and that nothing is missing.

The Right-Side-Up Pyramid

If the introduction of your essay looks like an upside-down pyramid, the conclusion looks like a pyramid right-side-up, with more specific information at the beginning and more general information at the end. Here's how:

The first sentence of the conclusion should restate the main idea.

There are plenty of reasons why cats make better pets than any other animals.

The next sentence should say something a little more general but still stay on the main idea.

Many people would be happy to have a cat.

The final sentence should wrap things up and finish the essay. It should be very general.

Pets such as cats help people all over the world live happier lives.

When you put your conclusion together, it will look like this:

There are plenty of reasons why cats make better pets than any other animals. Many people would be happy to have a cat. Pets such as cats help people all over the world live happier lives.

Writer's Handbook HB 25

Writing Poetry

Poetry is different from other forms of writing. Some poems are written in lines and stanzas and follow a rhyme or rhythm. Some poems are simply words or phrases with no rhyme. Most poems are full of imagery or word pictures. Whatever form a poem takes, it's one of the most creative forms of writing.

When you start to write a poem, the first thing to do is to pick a subject. It's a good idea to pick a subject that you know something about or a subject that means a lot to you. Next you should try to write down interesting ideas about your subject. You can write down your ideas however you like.

Then it is time to write your first draft. Once again, you can use any form you like to write your poem. Be sure to use plenty of descriptive words, or words that describe sounds, smells, tastes, and how things look and feel. As you begin to write, your poem might already be taking on its own form.

Revising is an important part of all writing, including writing poetry. You'll probably revise your poem many times. You might want to try changing the form of your poem. Once it's written, you may think it would be better stated in rhyme. You may think your poem is better if it doesn't rhyme. Just make sure your poem's message and ideas are clear to your readers.

Once you have written your final version, read it over to yourself. Then read it out loud. You may find more areas to improve.

Types of Poetry

Ballad: A ballad tells a story. Ballads are usually written as quatrains (four-line stanzas). Often, the first and third lines have four accented syllables; the second and fourth have three.

Blank Verse: Blank verse poems do not rhyme, but they have meter. Beginning with the second syllable of a line, every other syllable is accented.

Epic: An epic is a long poem that tells a story. The story describes adventures of heroes.

Free Verse: Free verse poems do not rhyme and do not have meter.

Haiku: Haiku is a form of poetry developed in Japan. The words of a haiku poem represent nature. A haiku is three lines in length. The first line is five syllables; the second is seven syllables; and the third is five syllables in length.

Limerick: A limerick is a funny poem that has five lines. Lines one, two, and five rhyme and have three stressed syllables. Lines three and four rhyme and have two stressed syllables.

Lyric: A lyric is a short poem that expresses personal feeling.

Ode: An ode is a long lyric. It expresses deeper feelings and uses poetic devices and imagery.

Sonnet: A sonnet is a fourteen-line poem that expresses personal feeling. Each line in a sonnet is ten syllables in length; every other syllable is stressed, beginning with the second syllable.

Poetry Terms

Alliteration: Alliteration is the repeating of the beginning consonant sounds:

cute, cuddly, calico cats

End Rhyme: End rhyme refers to the rhyming words at the ends of two or more lines of poetry:

Her favorite pastime was to take a **hike**.
His first choice was to ride a **bike**.

Foot: A foot is one unit of meter.

Meter: Meter is the pattern of accented and unaccented syllables in the lines of a traditional poem.

Onomatopoeia: Onomatopoeia is the use of a word whose sound makes you think of its meaning. Here are some examples:

bang, beep, buzz, clang, swish, thump, zoom

Quatrain: A quatrain is a four-line stanza:

At night she looks up at the stars
And thinks of what might be.
By day she works and studies so
To someday live her dreams.

Stanza: A stanza is a section in a poem named for the number of lines it contains.

Verse: Verse is a name for a line of traditional poetry.

Revising
Elaborate and Clarify

Thesaurus

When it comes to saying things in different, more interesting ways, the thesaurus is one of the best friends a writer can have.

A thesaurus is a reference book that lists the *synonyms* (words that have the same or similar meaning) of words, and the *antonyms* (words that have the opposite meaning) of words.

Many times writers get stuck using the same words over and over. It's difficult to think of new and more colorful words. The next time you are writing, ask yourself, "Have I used a word too many times? Is there a better way to say this?" Chances are, the answer will be yes. That's where a thesaurus can help.

For example, let's say you are writing a descriptive essay about a place, and you have picked a beach where you vacationed last summer. You have written that the ocean was **beautiful**. You have said that the sky was a **beautiful** shade of blue. You have stated that the tropical plants were **beautiful**. Do you see a pattern yet?

All those things were beautiful, but there are more colorful words you can use. Maybe the ocean is **stunning** or **spectacular**. The sky might be a **lovely** or even an **exquisite** shade of blue. And how about those tropical plants? Are they **extravagant, magnificent,** or **dramatic** in their beauty? Use rich words and your writing becomes truly **fabulous**.

Dictionary

One of the most helpful tools for writers is the dictionary. Just think of it! Every word you could possibly need is in there. Until now, you might have used your dictionary only to look up the spellings of difficult words. That's important because good spelling makes writing clearer, but it's not the only information in a dictionary.

Your dictionary contains valuable information, such as the history of words, a guide for pronunciation, foreign words and phrases, the names of historical people, the names of places in the world, and lots of other interesting things. Some dictionaries even contain the Declaration of Independence and the Constitution of the United States! The next time you are looking for more than just the spelling of a word, try your dictionary.

Web Sites

With the help of an adult, try these Web sites for even more help in building your vocabulary and making your writing richer and clearer.

http://www.writetools.com
This is a one-stop Web site for writers. It contains links to reference materials, almanacs, calendars, historical documents, government resources, grammar and style guides, and all kinds of other tools for writing and editing.

http://www.bartleby.com
This Web site has links to several on-line dictionaries, encyclopedias, thesauri, and many other useful and interesting sources. It also contains links to on-line fiction and nonfiction books. It's like having a library of your own.

Capitalization

Capitalize:

- the first word in a sentence.
- people's names and the names of particular places.
- titles of respect and titles that are part of names.
- initials of names.
- place names and words formed from them.
- the months of the year and the days of the week.
- important words in the names of groups.
- important words in the names of holidays.
- the first word in the greeting or closing of a letter.
- the word *I*.
- the most important words in a title.
- the first word in a direct quotation.

Sentence

A sentence is a group of words that tells a complete thought.
A sentence has two parts: a **subject** and a **predicate**.

- The complete subject tells who or what the sentence is about.
  The runners are ready.

- The complete predicate tells what happened.
  The people in the stands **watched excitedly**.

Subject-Verb Agreement

A subject and its verb must agree. Add *-s* or *-es* to a verb in the present tense when the subject is a singular noun or *he, she,* or *it*. Do not add *-s* if the subject is a plural noun or if the subject is *I, you, we,* or *they*.

My **sister reads** about urban wildlife in her social studies class.
The **students read** about how to protect the animals.
I like stories about the wildlife, too.

Abbreviations and Initials

Abbreviations are shortened forms of words. Many abbreviations begin with a capital letter and end with a period. An initial is the first letter of a name. An initial is written as a capital letter and a period.

Abbreviate:

- titles of address.
  Mister (Mr. Fred K. Mitchel)
  Mistress (Mrs. Janet Noda)
  Doctor (Dr. L. M. Roberto)
  Junior (Greg Ward, Jr.)

- words used in addresses.
  Street (St.)
  Avenue (Ave.)
  Route (Rte.)
  Boulevard (Blvd.)
  Road (Rd.)

- days of the week.
  Sunday (Sun.)
  Monday (Mon.)
  Tuesday (Tues.)
  Wednesday (Wed.)
  Thursday (Thurs.)
  Friday (Fri.)
  Saturday (Sat.)

- months of the year.
  January (Jan.)
  February (Feb.)
  March (Mar.)
  April (Apr.)
  August (Aug.)
  September (Sept.)
  October (Oct.)
  November (Nov.)
  December (Dec.)
  (May, June, and July do not have abbreviated forms.)

- directions.
  North (N)
  East (E)
  South (S)
  West (W)

Note: *Ms.* is a title of address used for women. It is not an abbreviation of *Mistress*, but it requires a period. (Ms. Lynn Murphy)

Quotation Marks

Quotation marks are used to separate a speaker's exact words from the rest of the sentence. Begin a **direct quotation** with a capital letter. Use a comma to separate the direct quotation from the speaker's name. When a direct quotation comes at the end of a sentence, put the end mark inside the last quotation mark. When writing a conversation, begin a new paragraph with each change of speaker. For example:

Elise said, "I'm going to adopt a kitten from the shelter." Elise had wanted a pet for a long time. Her parents thought she was ready to help take care of a pet.

"I'll go with you," said Jason. "I might find a cat or dog that I might like to adopt, too!"

End Marks

Every sentence must end with a **period,** an **exclamation point,** or a **question mark**.

- Use a **period** at the end of a statement or a command.
  Statement: My favorite colors are blue and green.
  Command: Please put on your life jacket before going in the lake.

- Use an **exclamation point** at the end of a firm command or at the end of a sentence that shows great feeling or excitement.
  Command: Watch out for the jellyfish!
  Exclamation: What a beautiful sunrise!

- Use a **question mark** at the end of an asking sentence.
  Question: How many colors are in a rainbow?

Commas

Commas in Sentences

Use a **comma**:

- after an introductory word in a sentence.
    Yes, Rebecca and Todd's wedding was beautiful!

- to separate items in a series.
    She carried white, yellow, and pink flowers.

- when speaking directly to a person.
    Laura, would you sing another song?

- to separate a direct quotation from the speaker's name.
    "I hope they take a lot of pictures," said Scott.

- with *and, or,* or *but* when combining sentences.
    Lynda liked spice cake best, but Chris preferred chocolate.

Commas in Letters

Use a **comma**:

- after the greeting and closing of a friendly letter.
    Dear Taylor,
    Yours truly, Hayley

- after the city and before the state in the heading of a letter.
    Columbus, OH

- after the day of the month and before the year in the heading of a letter.
    September 7, 2003

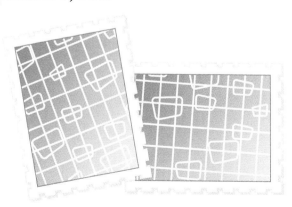

Parts of Speech

Nouns

- A **singular noun** names one person, place, or thing.
  boy   hillside   book

- A **plural noun** names more than one person, place, or thing.
  To make most singular nouns plural, add -*s*.
  boys   hillsides   books

- For nouns ending in *sh, ch, x,* or *z,* add -*es* to make the noun plural.
  brush/brushes   bunch/bunches   fox/foxes

- For nouns ending in a consonant and *y,* change the *y* to *i* and add -*es*.
  family/families

- For most nouns that end in *f* or *fe,* replace *f* or *fe* with *ves* to make the noun plural.
  wolf/wolves

- Some words change spelling when the plural is formed.
  man/men   child/children   person/people
  woman/women   mouse/mice   goose/geese

- Some words have the same singular and plural form.
  deer/deer   sheep/sheep   moose/moose

Verbs

- An **action verb** shows action in a sentence.
  We **study** many subjects in school.

- Sometimes a **helping verb** is needed to help the main verb show action. A helping verb comes before a main verb.
  We **will study** many new things this year.

- Verbs can tell about the **present,** the **past,** or the **future**.
  We **learn** about how to protect the environment.
  Last week, we **learned** about the rain forests.
  Next week, we **will learn** about protecting our oceans.

To show past action, -ed is added to most verbs. Verbs that do not add -ed are called **irregular** verbs.

Some common irregular verbs are:

Present	Past	With *have, has,* or *had*
bring	brought	brought
eat	ate	eaten
give	gave	given
go	went	gone
ring	rang	rung
take	took	taken

- A **linking verb** connects the subject of a sentence to a word or words in the predicate that tell about the subject. Linking verbs include *am, is, are, was,* and *were. Seem* and *become* are linking verbs, too.

Pronouns

A **pronoun** can replace a **noun** naming a person, place, or thing. Pronouns include *I, me, you, we, us, he, she, it, they,* and *them.*

- A pronoun may take the place of the subject of a sentence.
  Daryn likes to run, hike, and lift weights.
  He likes to run, hike, and lift weights.

- A pronoun may replace a noun that is the object of a preposition.
  Hanna threw the ball to **Lakesha**.
  Hanna threw the ball to **her**.

- A **demonstrative pronoun** talks about things that are either nearby or far away. Use *this* and *these* to talk about one or more things that are nearby.
  This is my favorite tennis racket.
  These are good shoes for running.

Use *that* and *those* to talk about things that are far away.
  That is a good place to watch the race.
  Those are new bleachers.

Adjectives

An **adjective** describes a noun or a pronoun.
> The mountains are **huge**.
> They are also **beautiful**.

Adverbs

An **adverb** is usually used to describe a verb.

- Many adverbs end in *-ly*.
> The family spoke **excitedly** of their vacation.

- *Very* is an adverb meaning "to a high degree" or "extremely."
Never use *real* in place of *very*.
> **Incorrect:** Tammy was *real* excited about the boat ride.
> **Correct:** Tammy was *very* excited about the boat ride.

Comparisons

- To compare two people, places, or things, add *-er* to most adjectives and adverbs.
> The chocolate milkshake is **thick**. That vanilla milkshake is **thicker**.

- To compare three or more items, add *-est* to most adjectives and adverbs.
> The strawberry milkshake is the **thickest**.

- The words *more* and *most* can also be used to compare two or more persons, places, or things.
> Rico is excited about helping with the project.
> Francis is **more** excited about helping with the project.
> Samantha is the **most** excited of all.

- Sometimes the words *good* and *bad* are used to compare. These words change forms in comparisons.
> This apple tastes **good**. The orange tastes **better**.
> The peaches are the **best**.
> The weather is **bad** today. It is going to be **worse** tomorrow. It is supposed to be the **worst** on Monday.

Note: Use *better* or *worse* to compare two things. Use *best* or *worst* to compare three or more things.

Prepositions

A **preposition** helps tell when, where, or how.

- Prepositions include the words *in, at, under,* and *over.*
  Miguel looked **at** the map.

Common Prepositions

about	beneath	inside	under
above	beside	near	underneath
across	between	of	until
after	beyond	off	unto
against	by	on	up
along	down	out of	upon
amid	during	outside	with
among	except	over	within
around	except for	through	without
before	for	till	
behind	from	to	
below	in	toward	

Conjunctions

The words *and, or,* and *but* are **conjunctions**.

- Conjunctions may be used to join words within a sentence.
  Miguel wanted to go to the mountains **and** the ocean.
  His father said they could go to the mountains **or** the ocean.
  The mountains are beautiful **but** far away.

- Conjunctions can be used to join two or more sentences.
  When using a conjunction to join sentences, put a comma
  before the conjunction.
  We can go for a jog on the beach**, or** we can play volleyball.
  Miguel wanted to jog**, but** Cynthia wanted to play volleyball.
  Miguel jogged**, and** Cynthia played volleyball.

Homophones

Some words sound alike but have different spellings and meanings. These words are called homophones.

- Here is a list of some homophones often confused in writing:

are	**Are** is a form of the verb *be*.
our	**Our** is a possessive noun.
hour	An **hour** is sixty minutes.
its	**Its** is a possessive pronoun.
it's	**It's** is a contraction of the words *it is*.
there	**There** means "in that place."
their	**Their** is a possessive pronoun. It shows something belongs to more than one person or thing.
they're	**They're** is a contraction made from the words *they are*.
two	**Two** is a number.
to	**To** means "toward."
too	**Too** means "also." It can also mean "more than enough."
your	**Your** is a possessive pronoun.
you're	**You're** is a contraction made from the words *you are*.

Signal Words

Signal words help writers move from one idea to another. Here is a list of some common signal words.

Time-Order Signal Words

after	first	later	next
before	meanwhile	immediately	when
during	until	finally	then

Comparison/Contrast Signal Words

in the same way	like	as well	also
but	however	otherwise	yet
still	even though	although	on the other hand

Concluding or Summarizing Signal Words

as a result	finally	in conclusion	to sum up
therefore	lastly	in summary	all in all

Listening, Speaking, and Thinking Skills

Listening

These tips will help you be a good listener:

- Listen carefully when others are speaking.

- Keep in mind your reason for listening. Are you listening to learn about a topic? To be entertained? To get directions? Decide what you should get out of the listening experience.

- Look directly at the speaker. Doing this will help you concentrate on what he or she has to say.

- Do not interrupt the speaker or talk to others while the speaker is talking.

- Ask questions when the speaker is finished talking if there is anything you did not understand.

Speaking

These guidelines can help you become an effective speaker.

Giving Oral Reports

- Be prepared. Know exactly what you are going to talk about and how long you will speak. Have your notes in front of you.

- Speak slowly and clearly. Speak loudly enough so everyone can hear you.

- Look at your audience.

Taking Part in Discussions

- Listen to what others have to say.

- Disagree politely. Let others in the group know you respect their points of view.

- Try not to interrupt others. Everyone should have a chance to speak.

Thinking

Writers use a variety of thinking skills as they work through the writing process. These skills include **logic, analyzing, setting goals, creativity,** and **problem solving**. As you write, keep these skills in mind and try to put them to use as much as possible.

- **Logic** Writers use logic to support a point of view by using reasoning, facts, and examples.

- **Analyzing** Analyzing is a thinking skill that requires the writer to think about and examine the information learned about a topic. Once the information is examined, a general conclusion or more meaningful understanding can be made about the topic.

- **Setting Goals** When setting goals, writers must think about deadlines (when the assignment is due; how much time there is for prewriting, drafting, revising, editing, and publishing), the objective of the writing assignment, and the amount of research required.

- **Creativity** Using creativity means using the imagination. Writers let their minds wonder about many different ways to tackle an assignment before finally settling on one. It is often necessary to start an assignment, stop, try it a different way, stop again, and maybe even go back to the original idea. Thinking creatively and openly allows the writer to examine many options.

- **Problem Solving** Learning to problem solve helps writers make decisions about the writing assignment and helps them use facts and opinions correctly. Strategies for problem solving include: naming the problem; thinking of everything about the problem; thinking of ways to solve the problem; choosing the best plan to solve the problem and trying it out; and analyzing the result.

Publishing Share

This is the last step of the writing process. You have gathered and organized information. You have drafted, revised, and edited your writing. Your project is completed. Here are some tips for publishing your work.

Ways to Publish

There are lots of ways to publish your work. Keep your audience in mind as you choose different publishing methods. Your teacher might ask you to publish your work by writing your final draft on a clean piece of paper, with a title and your name at the top. You might try one of the publishing methods from this book, like an author's circle or a letter with an addressed envelope. It all depends on who is going to read or listen to your work.

Using a Computer

Computers can be very helpful when it comes to publishing. If you use a computer to publish your writing, try these helpful hints:

- Use a bigger type for the title of your work than for the body.

- Use a different type for the title of your work than for the body.

- Use the "spell check" feature to help you make sure you have spelled everything correctly. Be careful, though. This feature is great at catching real spelling mistakes, but it can't tell the difference between *there* and *their* or other homophones.

- You can also use a computer to add pictures, graphs, tables, or charts to your published work.

When it comes to using a computer to publish, check with your teacher, a parent, or another responsible adult first.

Publishing by Hand

Here are some suggestions for publishing without a computer.

- Check with your teacher for guidelines about printing or cursive writing.

- Remember, handwriting counts! You want your audience to be able to read what you publish. Make it clear, neat, and large enough to read.

- Use lined paper if you are publishing by hand. That way, your writing will stay neat.

- Use dark ink when publishing by hand. Try a pen with eraseable ink. That way, if you make a mistake, you don't have to rewrite the entire piece.

- Try using a fine-point marker or colored pencil to decorate the title of your work.

- Try stencils or stamps for some decorative touches when publishing by hand.

As always, check with your teacher for guidelines for publishing by hand.